PERGAMON INSTITUTE OF ENGLISH

English Language Teaching Documents

General Editor: C. J. BRUMFIT

VIDEO APPLICATIONS IN ENGLISH LANGUAGE TEACHING

The British Council ELT Documents — Back Issues

document no.	title
77/1	*Games, Simulation and Role Playing*
102	*English as an International Language*
104	*Developments in the Training of Teachers of English*
105	*The Use of Media in ELT*
106	*Team Teaching in ESP*
108	*National Syllabuses*
109	*Study Modes and Academic Development of Overseas Students*
110	*Focus on the Teacher—Communicative Approaches to Teacher Training*
111	*Issues in Language Testing*
112	*The ESP Teacher: Role, Development and Prospects*
113	*Humanistic Approaches—An Empirical View*

Special Issues and Occasional Papers

1. *The Foreign Language Learning Process*
2. *The Teaching of Comprehension*
3. *Projects in Materials Design*
4. *The Teaching of Listening Comprehension Skills*

VIDEO APPLICATIONS
IN
ENGLISH LANGUAGE TEACHING

Edited by

JOHN McGOVERN

British Council, Jordan

ELT Documents 114

Published in association with
THE BRITISH COUNCIL
by
PERGAMON PRESS

Oxford · New York · Toronto · Sydney · Paris · Frankfurt

U.K	Pergamon Press Ltd., Headington Hill Hall, Oxford OX3 0BW, England
U.S.A.	Pergamon Press Inc., Maxwell House, Fairview Park, Elmsford, New York 10523, U.S.A.
CANADA	Pergamon Press Canada Ltd., Suite 104, 150 Consumers Road, Willowdale, Ontario M2J 1P9, Canada
AUSTRALIA	Pergamon Press (Aust.) Pty. Ltd., P.O. Box 544, Potts Point, N.S.W. 2011, Australia
FRANCE	Pergamon Press SARL, 24 rue des Ecoles, 75240 Paris, Cedex 05, France
FEDERAL REPUBLIC OF GERMANY	Pergamon Press GmbH, Hammerweg 6, D-6242 Kronberg-Taunus, Federal Republic of Germany

First edition 1983

Library of Congress Cataloging in Publication Data

Main entry under title:
Video applications in English language teaching.
(English language teaching documents; 114)
1. English language—Study and teaching—Audio-visual instruction—Addresses, essays, lectures.
I. Brumfit, Christopher. II. British Council.
III. Series.
PE1067.V5 1983 428'.007'1 82-25058

British Library Cataloguing in Publication Data

Video applications in English language: teaching.
—(English language teaching documents; 114)
1. English language—Audio-visual instruction
I. Brumfit, C. J. II. Series
371.3'33 LB1043.5

ISBN 0-08-029476-6

Printed in Great Britain by A. Wheaton & Co. Ltd., Exeter

PREFACE

It is appropriate that the first issue of *ELT Documents* to be published by Pergamon Press should be on the use of video in the English language classroom. Not only is video a major technical innovation, the uses of which for language teaching have still to be predicted and explored, but it is also an innovation that is likely to have a major social impact on education at large.

One of the main aims of *ELT Documents* is to explore and comment on the implications of general educational innovations for English language teaching throughout the world. The use of video remains still a contentious issue. It is by no means clear—yet—that it will not follow the fate of language laboratories and distract teachers from a central concern for their relationship with students and the language which results from that relationship. It has taken many years of experimentation with language laboratories for their uses to be humanized. The papers offered here illustrate that many writers are aware of such potential problems and are anxious to accommodate video within the mainstream of language teaching. They also show a concern for the link between principles and practice which is essential for the well-being of the profession.

It is appropriate, too, that this collection was assembled by the British Council, who were responsible for previous issues of the journal. We hope that through the British Council, and other organizations with firm links overseas and in the classroom, the practical activities of teachers may be reported and discussed in relation to current general principles. All this should be part of the continuous professional debate through which improvement of our practice and clarification of our thinking must develop.

There is another sense in which this topic provides us with a convenient starting point, for video raises in a particularly strong form one of the major socially created difficulties for teachers in general and language teachers in particular, at least within British law. This is the question of copyright. The copyright law in Britain is just about to be reformed, but unfortunately the reforms seem to be motivated more by commercial instincts than by educational ones. In practice, many educational institutions have copied—often illegally—both printed material and video material. The crucial question professionally is whether education will be improved by an insistence that all material which is in copyright should actually be paid for, when there is no question whatsoever of anyone making money out of the copying. The copying of *textbooks* specifically designed for education is, of course, another matter.

There are two kinds of acceptable copying. Many copyright materials—poems, extracts from contemporary writings, academic writings, clips from films and television—are essential for an education which is not solely historical in approach. On the other hand, there are also copyright materials which may be cited for their linguistic or other value, quite independently of their original purpose. The first type of copying is frequently attacked, but it does in fact provide a form of free publicity. Every student who is exposed to a piece of commercial material in the classroom (provided that sources are conscientiously stated) is given information which creates a market for either the original product or others like it. No publisher, as far as we know, has ever offered a fee to teachers for this publicity—yet we should be very clear that there is just as much evidence for the view that this copying contributes to the sale of goods as there is for the frequently-asserted belief that those who are exposed to copyright educational material would otherwise be willing and able to pay for it themselves. The choice in practice, for most people, is between 'pirating' and no contact at all with certain ideas or creative materials.

The second type of copying raises an even more ridiculous issue. It is illegal to record substantial tracts of television and to use them as instances of language. Yet such quotation has absolutely no commercial implications, and refusal to allow it prevents a great deal of effective language and cultural work from taking place. Restrictions on the free flow of ideas and images, for non-commercial purposes, can only be anti-educational and anti-democratic. It is extraordinary that no substantial lobby has developed to attack the commercial selfishness of both the existing copyright law, and the proposed revisions.

C J Brumfit

CONTENTS

VIDEO AND ENGLISH LANGUAGE TEACHING IN BRITAIN

FRANCES MACKNIGHT

Introduction

This article examines video in the context of English language teaching (ELT) in Britain. Its aim is to provide answers to the 'wh' questions of video in English language teaching, viz; how many institutions have invested in video; why they have done so; what type of hardware and software they use; who they use it with; how they use it and what the main problems of using video are. The information is based on data drawn from the results of a short initial survey, followed by a detailed questionnaire for video owners only, administered to members of the Association of Recognized English Language Schools and English language teaching units within tertiary institutions, between August, 1979 and March, 1980.

1. How Many Institutions Have Invested in Video?

Institutions	+ Video		– Video	
	No	%	No	%
Total	82	61	52	39
Schools	41	48	44	52
Universities	16	84	3	16
Further Education	25	83	5	17

Table 1. *Extent of Video Implantation in ELT*

Table 1 shows that 61% of institutions have so far invested in video, i.e. most of the public sector (mainly composed of English language teaching units in tertiary institutions) and just under half of the private sector (largely represented by independent language schools). Size of institution is not a relevant factor in video acquisition.

For a more detailed account see MacKnight, F. R. (1981) *Review and Analysis of Present Video use in EFL Teaching*, M.Ed., University of Wales.

2. Why Do Institutions Invest in Video?

The factors that influence investment in video are essentially non-linguistic. Occasionally video is inherited: 'just there' for no particular reason, or it was simply an impulse buy. A major factor in a competitive teaching industry is the prestige thought to surround video ownership. The latter can be interpreted as the hallmark of a progressive institution. Personal contacts influence acquisition: a positive experience of video in one institution leads to its installation in another. Video is often perceived as a useful time shift extension of television and (despite the 1956 Copyright Law) is acquired particularly for the access it gives to specialized interest off-air recordings. Video is also obtained in order to expand aspects of the curriculum, especially teacher training and Specific English programmes, after which its use is frequently extended to general interest courses. Video is commonly introduced to give a lift to methodology in terms of interest and motivation, to extend the range of teaching techniques available, e.g. to enable more sophisticated presentations, and to add an extra dimension to course design e.g. by expanding the content and type of skills capable of being developed.

While linguistic factors are a minor element in video acquisition, the main linguistic benefit is considered to be the presentation of chunks of authentic language within a whole context, thus enabling the student to experience authentic language in a controlled environment. Video can literally provide the complete picture: listening comprehension reinforced by watching comprehension. Video is considered *potentially* capable of developing a wide range of linguistic and semi-linguistic skills e.g. highlighting language functions, pinpointing non-verbal signals, showing the relationship between linguistic and paralinguistic features. This potential, however, is perceived as a beneficial side-effect and future possibility rather than a reason for investing in video.

3. What Type of Hardware do Institutions Use?

2%	JVC UMATIC
8%	BAIRD VHS
8%	SONY BETAMAX
8%	JVC VHS
8%	PHILIPS 1700
10%	PANASONIC VHS
25%	PHILIPS 1500
31%	SONY-UMATIC
	Open Reel only
	*Other

*Other = Video shared with other departments, no control over format used.

Table 2. *Distribution of VCR Formats used*

The rapid advance of video technology is roughly reflected in the hardware institutions have. Table 2 shows that, where there is control over the type of machine chosen, virtually all institutions prefer VCR (video cassette recorder). Only a very small group continue to rely exclusively on open reel. Sony-Umatic is most popular, followed by Philips 1500. Both these machines are designed for the industrial and education markets. The newer formats aimed at the domestic market have, however, made rapid progress in a comparatively short time. Unfortunately there is no indication of the popularity of the Philips 2000 format, which had not been released during the period covered by the questionnaire. In common with other subject areas, ELT exhibits some multiple format use, with up to three different formats being used by the same institution. The education sector as a whole tends to buy video equipment outright, but 40% of ELT institutions rent their VCR and TV receiver/monitor. Renting is flexible and enables institutions to keep up with technological developments. Most rental agreements include servicing and in difficult repair cases an alternative VCR is substituted.

Taking the dates of equipment acquisitions as a guide to ELT interest in video, Table 3 indicates that interest was highest between 1976/78, with the level of VCR acquisitions being maintained in 1979. There was a predictable shift from open reel VTR (video tape recorder) to the more convenient and reliable VCR and from black and white to colour. Interest in the video camera has gradually increased and, as with VCRs, there is the beginning of a trend towards colour. By the period 1976/78 the black and white single camera was fairly well established. It is still the most widely used camera type, but has recently been overshadowed by the more mobile and flexible portapak. Camera users are present in a minority, (39% of all institutions: schools 57%, FE 30% and universities 13%) but of the institutions that planned to extend their video facilities (38%) just under half intended to add a camera to their resources in 1980. Other ways of expanding facilities included the addition of VCRs, monitors, and, in a small number of cases, editing facilities and a TV projection screen. There was one example of a purpose built studio. Institutions use camera types in various combinations, e.g. a tertiary ELT unit may have access to a shared media centre and in some cases, its own camera; schools generally have a single camera, and very occasionally, a studio. Approximately half of all institutions, however, rely exclusively on a single camera. Despite a gradual increase in camera acquisition, and a maintaining of interest in the VCR, the occurrence of editing facilities is very rare. The cost of this type of equipment is still well beyond most ELT users.

4. What Type of Software do Institutions Use?

The software available for ELT falls into four broad categories: (1) off-air recording from TV, (2) published ELT series, (3) commercially produced material apart from that shown on TV and (4) in-house productions. Off-air software is most widely used, (by 91% of institutions) and Table 4, outlines the kind of recordings used.

Date of Acquisition	Type of Video Equipment										
	TV Receiver			Video Recorder			Camera (excluding Studio Camera)				
							Single Camera		Portapak		
	B & W	Colour	Total	VTR Open Reel	VCR	Total	B & W	Colour	B & W	Colour	Total
Pre-1976	17	17	34	16	11	27	25				25
1976–78	9	37	46	9	32	41	31	6	6		43
1979	2	18	20	2	30	32	6	3	13	10	32
Total	28	72	100	27	73	100	62	9	19	10	100

Table 3. *Analysis of Video Equipment Acquisitions (showing percentage acquired of each type)*

Material	% of Institutions using this type
News and Documentary	86
Education	66
General Entertainment	43
Advertisements	27

Table 4. *Off-Air Software in ELT*

In the case of Specific English, the choice of off-air material is governed by its bearing on subject area e.g. medicine, maritime studies, and for General English by its topicality and relation to students' present interests. Software libraries are largely composed of off-air material, without which there would be a decline in video use. Compared to their counterparts abroad, British ELT institutions are fortunate in having access to English medium TV, which provides the bulk of video software. However, many of these institutions consistently break the Copyright Law in making off-air recordings. ELT series, which are not shown on British TV, but may feature on networks abroad, are little used. The most often quoted series is *Bellcrest*, the video component of which is available in 15% of institutions. Non-televised commercially produced material, e.g. management training videos, is very rarely used. The production of in-house material depends on camera ownership, and is therefore limited. Material consists almost entirely of small scale productions of examples of student interaction, e.g. seminar discussions, interviews, role play. Examples of larger scale projects include a comparison of interview techniques, documentaries based on topics of interest, specialist discussions, situational clips based on structures to be taught and examples of language functions in action.

5. Who is Video Used With?

This depends on student interest and level, the intensity and duration of the course, the availability of appropriate software and the interest in video of the individual teacher. Video is used with a wide range of students, (from air traffic controllers to diplomats) but four main groups can be distinguished:

(1) general interest students (72%),
(2) businessmen (49%),
(3) engineers (31%),
(4) tertiary level students, the majority of whom have a technical/scientific orientation (26%).

Categories inevitably overlap and only a general indication of student type is possible. Video is rather more often used with specific interest than general interest groups. It features most commonly at advanced level (91%), but is also fairly widely used at intermediate level (70%). It is unusual to find video being used with elementary students (36%). Video is more likely to be used with full time than part time students; it is rare to find video being used with students following courses where English is a subsidiary or enabling component within a broader programme e.g. courses geared to secretarial, business or academic qualifications. The camera parallels the VCR in the kind of students it is used with. Although occasionally used with general students, it is most commonly used with full time specific interest students, particularly those on business and other vocationally oriented courses. The size of group that watches video varies from one to thirty five, but over a third of institutions use video with groups of twelve.

6. How do Institutions Use Video?

This is considered under the following headings: Video material in the context of the course; the function video material fulfils and the skills it can help to develop; video material in the context of the lesson and a general perspective on the main characteristics of use.

Features of Video Component Use		Patterns 1	2	3	4	5
Video	Optional	+		+		
use	Obligatory		+		+	+
Nature of	Supplementary	+	+	+	+	
video material	Integral					+
Relationship of video	Not directly related	+	+			
material to other	Directly related			+	+	
Course Content	Essential					+
Occurrence of Patterns		43%	14%	44%	25%	39%

Table 5. *The Place of Video on the English Language Course*

Within the language course as a whole the video element may be optional or obligatory, supplementary or integral, and indirectly related, directly related, or essential, to other course content. Table 5 indicates that video material is generally optional and supplementary and as often unrelated as related to the rest of the course. Video is seldom co-ordinated with other teaching aids, although a few examples are given of its use with audiocassette, language laboratory and print material in the form of textbooks, off-prints and video transcripts. A significant minority of institutions (39%) use video as an essential part of some of their courses, although exclusively integrative use is very rare. The video element is most integrated, and therefore most important, on business oriented courses. It is also prominent on other types of vocationally oriented courses, e.g. programmes for doctors, technicians, youth hostel wardens. It is used to some extent on study skills programmes, particularly those with a science and technology bias. There is a high correlation between integrative video use and the availability of camera and editing facilities. These resources enhance the versatility of video, extending it beyond being merely a time shift mechanism for TV and enabling material to be more easily fitted to student needs.

Functions naturally vary according to type of student group and course objectives, but Table 6 indicates the main functions that video material is at present thought to fulfil.

Functions	% of occurrence
Introduction to topic/stimulus of interest	89
Information on cultural background	75
General language spin off	61
Consolidation of known language	48
Contextualization of new language	45
Identification and practice of language items	45
Development of professional competence	36
Basis for project work	27
Self analysis of professional task	20
Development of social competence	16
Self analysis of social task	16
Other	
Literary background and enrichment	
Literacy training	
Familiarization with new procedures/techniques	
Entertainment	

Table 6. *Functions which Video Material Fulfils*

Video is most widely used to introduce and stimulate interest in a topic, to give information on cultural background and for general language spin-off. This is generally interpreted as the development of listening skills, and indicates a belief that something useful can always be picked up from video. Just under half of the institutions find video useful for reviewing and introducing language items in context. Video is also found useful for developing professional competence but is little used for developing social competence. Models of professional competence are generally easier to isolate and identify and set up in a realistic way. They also allow for less deviation from the norm than social behaviour. A camera extends the range of video functions. It is useful for developing professional and social competence and essential for student analyses of their own performance; feedback is a function ideally suited to video. Just over a quarter of institutions use video as a basis for project work, mostly as a stimulus and jump-off point. In a few exceptional cases video is part of the project itself, with a video camera under student control: e.g. foreign doctors on placement who made a record of their experiences; general students who made a short documentary. Despite the time and organization involved in such projects, the few institutions that have attempted this application have found it worthwhile. Entertainment is classified as a function by some users and as an incidental benefit by others.

Skills	% of institutions using video to develop these skills
*Extensive listening	75
Intensive listening	73
Interpretation of non-verbal signals	45
Oral Production	43
Student awareness of progress towards target language behaviour	41
Writing	25
Extensive reading	11

*Where both intensive and extensive listening are cited, video is used more frequently for the latter.

Table 7. *Skills which Video Material is used to Develop*

Video is of course used to develop different skills at different times, and in addition, any rigid division of skills is artificial. Nevertheless, Table 7 illustrates that video is found most helpful in developing aural/oral skills, particularly listening skills. Video is also used to heighten awareness of non-verbal signals and appropriate behaviour. Interpreting language skills in the broadest sense, video is considered useful for stimulating the ability to interpret the interaction of receptive and productive skills within a total context, and to act appropriately. This alerting of powers of observation and assimilation may be termed *affective* skills. Video is occasionally used as a stimulus to practising reading and writing skills, but is not thought to be particularly useful in these areas.

The way the video component is handled within the lesson naturally varies widely, depending on the student group, the type of video material and the function it is expected to fulfil. Virtually all institutions however, introduce and follow up video material.

The main ways in which institutions back up video material are shown in Table 8. Where deductive reasoning is being developed, students may go straight into video, without any introduction e.g. doctors diagnosing complaints. Activity simultaneous with watching video is less widespread. It demands a certain level of proficiency to carry out several tasks concurrently, but, where students can cope, a simultaneous activity prompts alertness and focuses attention. Introductory and follow up activities are sometimes more wishful thinking than always systematically carried out, but everyone is aware of the need for support material. Doubts are candidly expressed about the pious hope that students will learn something merely by watching video.

The lesson time occupied by the video component varies considerably, but broad patterns can be identified. With advanced and intermediate groups the average length of video shown is from 20 to 40 minutes, and with elementary groups from 10 to 20 minutes. Short sequences of 5 minutes or less are rare,

Stage	% of occurrence	Activity	% of occurrence
		Oral indication of main theme	75
		Introduction of difficult lexis and structures	59
		Oral summary of content	39
		Written summary of content	9
		Other:	
Introduction	95	Prediscussion of topic	
		Enacting of related simulation/role play and checking of hypotheses against video version	
		Pre-teaching of language functions to be seen	
		Setting of pointer questions to focus attention on important points	
		Specification of target task on completion of viewing process	
		Orientation by watching slide extracts from video material to be seen	
		Fill in a worksheet	39
Parallel with watching video	52	Take formal notes i.e. basis of summary, guide to composition, stimulus to free creative writing	27
		Draw/complete a diagram	9
		Discussion	89
		Written exercise e.g. precis/summary, cloze type exercises, worksheet completion, reports and criticisms, reviews, guided composition, free writing	52
		Role play	43
		Reading related text	34
		Dialogue practice	23
Follow-up	100	Structure practice	20
		Other:	
		Oral summary	
		Comprehension check through question and answer process	
		Improvization and dramatization of a related theme	
		Presentation of related technical material	
		Making a film on similar theme	

Table 8. *Exploitation of Video Material within the lesson*

and some very long sequences are quoted e.g. up to an hour for advanced students and 45 minutes for intermediate students. A video shown in class may be a complete unit in itself (of whatever length) or part of a longer original from which it has been extracted. A video is generally shown in its original entirety, with approximately a quarter of institutions extracting shorter sequences from longer originals. At advanced level the average video component occupies half to two thirds of teaching time, half the teaching unit at intermediate level, and approximately a quarter at elementary level.

There appears to be a gradual increase in frequency of video use. The majority of institutions use video occasionally, i.e. once per 40/50 course hours, which in most cases means about once a fortnight.

On some specific interest courses however, video may be used up to once per 5 or 6 hours. Frequency of use is influenced by variables similar to those that affect the types of student group with whom video is used. Video use may be concentrated at one stage of the course only, or used at regular intervals throughout.

7. Some Conclusions

All seems fairly well with video. Implantation is at a respectable level; use is gradually increasing; video has an important role on certain types of course, fulfils a range of functions and develops some useful skills. Closer examination, however, reveals widespread lack of use. Extent of implantation is not a reliable guide to use and at least a third of institutions underutilize video: "Whatever we've got, we don't use it much." Lack of use also extends to the video camera. Eight institutions have a camera facility which they never use. The pool of video users is therefore smaller than figures might suggest. While video is used integratively by a small group of institutions, mainly but not entirely with an orientation to specific interests, it has an important role only in a minority of cases. It is a supplementary element rather than an essential part of the language course. It remains a largely peripheral resource, unco-ordinated with other aids. There is a marked tendency to treat video as a pleasant optional extra, a 'Friday afternoon treat', Video is under-exploited: "Although we have video we don't really exploit it". Frequency of use does not necessarily mean variety of exploitation. The potential of video is far from being realized and it is capable of more functions that it generally fulfils, particularly those of a more strictly linguistic nature. In terms of skills video is used most to develop the listening skill in isolation, often more as an extended audiotape than as the means of giving a more complete idea of language in action in the framework of a complete situation. Despite interest in video and frequent references to its potential, there is an uncomfortable gap between actual and ideal use. Institutions generally acknowledge that video is not used as much or as constructively as it should be.

There is confusion about the aims of video use and uncertainty about what video can do. Institutions often have little idea what to use video *for*: "We use it just for whatever . . ."; "We don't use video to *specifically* teach anything". The problem seems particularly acute in general teaching contexts. It is unusual to find a systematic approach to video exploitation, which is characteristically fragmentary and largely depends on interested individuals working in isolation. It is common to discover that institutions have no particular policy of video use and organization of the video facility is often haphazard. In an appreciable number of cases there is no-one at all in charge of the video facility, and where an organizational framework exists it is more often for hardware than for software. Despite awareness of the present muddled situation, little concerted attempt has yet been made to rationalize it.

What are the main problems involved in video use? The disappointing extent of constructive video use and the general confusion surrounding applications are caused by a complex of interrelated problems, not all of which are within the control of the user. They can be summarized as problems related to software, over rapid technological development, costs in the broadest sense, organization and logistics and teacher training.

Despite an apparently wide range of software, particular difficulties are attached to each type. ELT series are part of a package, some of which may not be required, and it may be difficult to use an episode on a one-off basis. They are comparatively expensive to buy or hire and it becomes very costly to use only an extract. Many ELT series were originally made for a TV audience of language learners, with a consequent emphasis on redundancy and reinforcement, which makes them less suitable for classroom use. (This is gradually changing, however, as an increase of video use in foreign language teaching influences the style of TV presentations.) Non-broadcast commercial training material has a limited appeal, often being unsuitable for general or less advanced students, and it requires much adaptation for ELT. It is expensive to buy or hire and information on the type of material available is not readily accessible. In-house material depends on camera ownership and requires tight organization, time, and a level of skill that only a minority of institutions command. The camera itself tends to be underused, and when it is exploited, it is for small scale productions. Producers of in-house material do not intend to expand the volume and type of their output, even where suitable facilities exist because of time constraints.

Off-air material has the advantage of being free, (apart from the cost of a TV licence) offers a range of high quality, professionally presented material and is readily accessible; it is hardly surprising, therefore, that most institutions rely on off-air software, despite the fact that this often means infringing copyright. A dependence on off-air material however, makes video essentially synonymous with using authentic material, in the sense of any material not specifically designed for the language learner. (A TV script, or semi-scripted performance is not of course 'authentic' in the sense of using spontaneous language.) Authentic materials create problems of teaching and methodology. Choice of material is inevitably governed by area of interest rather than linguistic considerations, and where subject content is considered particularly useful, the audio element may be discounted. Ideally, off-air material can rarely be used 'straight', but the majority of institutions do not have the time or facilities to adapt it.

Help for the student is not built into authentic material, but has to come from the way the teacher presents and exploits it, and support material for student and teacher is generally essential. The richness and density of information conveyed by authentic material takes longer to absorb than ELT specific material and allowance has to be made for this in lesson pacing. It also makes authentic material hard to use with elementary learners. Students accustomed to learning from audio material may need special help. As a teaching aid, video involves a delicate balance between maintaining interest, going too fast for adequate comprehension, and becoming boring through repetition. In order to avoid the danger of video taking over a lesson, the staging of material needs careful handling if an acceptable balance is to be achieved between the video component and the teaching unit as a whole. In a situation where video is most used with advanced students, for up to an hour at a time, passivity is almost inevitable, and the task of maintaining student involvement stretches the teacher's powers of observation and sensitivity to classroom atmosphere. Video demands much time and energy; at least one of the reasons why discussion is such a popular follow-up is that it demands least effort in terms of teaching and materials preparation. In the present software situation video is a particularly exacting aid to use well. It is far from being a soft option or 'not really teaching,' as is sometimes believed.

The majority of institutions are dissatisfied with the present software situation. The most pressing need is for general interest material, which includes general, business and study skills interest. Alternative software is needed for all levels, but particularly for elementary students, and shorter sequences are required, from two to twenty minutes long, depending on level. The discrepancy between lengths of video requested and those actually used, suggests that many institutions rely on unadapted off-air material for lack of any convenient alternative. Whilst the debate continues on the merits of ELT specific and authentic materials (used in the sense of spontaneous language), the majority of institutions state a need for 'snippets of authentic language at work in a wide variety of situations', that can easily be slotted in to the language programme and there is a reaction against a 'set piece' structurally based approach. While an amateur approach is accepted for in-house material, it is not tolerated for commercial material as the user has become accustomed to a free supply of high quality off-air material. The market for alternative software depends on a maximum cost to the consumer of £50 per one to two hour tape which contains a range of professionally presented short items of an authentic nature.

Unfortunately the prospect of such alternative software becoming a reality is remote; any moves towards plugging the software gap are in the more established area of teacher training. There are few publishers with the requisite expertise and prospective publishers are deterred by the difficulties of the ELT market. The latter is in flux and it is difficult to establish its type and extent. The market research necessary would be slow and expensive. The market is limited, but has to be viable financially and is therefore considered on a global basis, which does not sufficiently allow for variations in local teaching and learning styles. The general English market is large but ill defined; the specific interest market more defined but fragmented. The kind of material required needs more definition before a publisher will take a gamble and users themselves are not clear about their precise software requirements. The consumer wants a polished product without being prepared to pay a high price, particularly in the case of general interest off-the-shelf cassettes. Until video is an essential course element, however, a supply of pre-recorded software will not be forthcoming. On the other hand, the move to video as an important aid would be accelerated if less time and energy were needed to accommodate it.

Copyright problems further restrict the type of software available. The 1956 Copyright Law predates video and is full of anomalies. There are no restrictions on Open University, education or in-house materials, but other categories cannot be recorded without permission from the holders of copyright and performers' rights for the component parts of the material. This involves a complex of rights and is unworkable. Another difficulty is the ownership rights of material produced by teachers in the course of their work, a difference that exists between schools and higher or further education, both categories into which ELT institutions fall. In addition, material copied under licence should not be retained for longer than a year, although the usefulness of material often outlasts this period. The majority of ELT users ignore copyright restrictions, copying non-education material, retaining it for long periods and, in some cases, sending it abroad. As this is a relatively small problem, broadcasting authorities turn a blind eye to infringements, but the longer the situation continues, the more difficult it will be to change it. The ELT user at present has little choice if he is to get value from his hardware; there is no deliberate intent to deprive producers and performers of their rights.

On balance, rapid technological development has benefited ELT, but it also contributes, to some extent, to the problems surrounding video use. The spread of technology is uneven, e.g. not all institutions have a freeze frame; the audio dub facility is not a feature of all VCRs, and editing suites are rare. Equipment becomes obsolete faster and the user cannot assimilate developments. A trend towards multiple format use makes cassette distribution more difficult, which in turn limits software developments. The complexity of technology may inhibit; teachers seem more willing to operate a single camera or portapak in preference to a studio camera. Finally, ELT is a spin-off market and equipment is rarely designed with the ELT user in mind. It would be helpful, for example, if the rewind mechanisms were more precise, portapaks were truly portable and master tapes were particularly strong.

Video is costly in terms of time, personnel, maintenance, and to some extent, finance. All aspects of its use are time-consuming. It is labour intensive: personnel are required to organize hardware and software, train teachers, and plan and teach material; in-house production is a team effort. Hardware has to be regularly maintained if it is to function smoothly and tapes may be stockpiled, thus freezing an asset. Apart from the high cost of editing facilities, which limits the adaptation of material to fit more closely to student needs, financial considerations are not a major factor. Nevertheless, video equipment is relatively expensive, and this may weigh more heavily as economic factors become more important.

Poor organization and complex logistics exacerbate the difficulties inherent in video use. Video rarely has a defined place in the hierarchy of responsibility and the onus for its use falls mostly on the uncoordinated efforts of interested individuals, who fit video work on top of the normal workload, often without allowance being made for the time involved. Video is not generally timetabled on a regular basis and some administrative upheaval may ensue while arrangements are made for hardware and students to be in the same place at the right time. Inefficient channels of organization and communication greatly hinder use.

Present software limitations mean that video material rarely appears on a schedule of work as do more established materials. The teacher has to take the initiative in deciding whether video would be useful, ascertain if relevant material exists, and well in advance of projected use, pick out a suitable extract from the corpus. As most material is recorded off-air, arrangements then have to be made for material to be recorded, after which it is assessed for suitability, and in an ideal world, support materials are prepared for teachers and students, and the material integrated with the language programme. Finally the material has to be taught, allowing for the attendant difficulties of authentic material. Once the teaching unit is complete, the success of the video component should be monitored and the material stored for easy retrieval. Even with efficient organization, this process is daunting. When it is left to one individual, it is hardly surprising that video is underused. Video use in these conditions resembles an obstacle race that only the most motivated can complete.

Despite widespread reliance on interested individuals for video exploitation, their interest remains largely unchannelled. Most institutions give informal help with the mechanical aspects of video, but systematic training in the construction and exploitation of video material is very rare. Teacher training is hardly ever organized on a compulsory basis, nor are teachers' guidance notes usually supplied. Teacher training is hindered by the lack of organization associated with video, the relatively small number per staff interested in video, and the small staffs characteristic of ELT units in tertiary institutions. There is little opportunity to try out video techniques across courses similar in level and content, and video is largely perceived as a fringe aid, which is not used on a regular basis. Where training *is* given, it is provided because in a given case video has a particularly important role, or because of the complexity of specific interest material. Teacher training is not used as a means of promoting more efficient video use: the need for teacher training is acknowledged, but confusion about the contribution video can make, and lack of experience with video as a classroom aid, inhibit experiment. As there is no established body of video methodology to build on, any training course would depart from traditional ideas of the transfer of knowledge from the initiated to the uninitiated. However teacher trainers with a knowledge of both hardware and ELT are hard to find, a problem rooted in the omission from past ELT courses of training in the manipulation and exploitation of audio visual material.

In light of the problems that at present beset video use, it may seem tempting to abandon it. However, the visual element in language teaching has proven value and video can greatly contribute to the development of professional, social and affective competence, and through the feedback facility, to an objective approach to language study. Although video is an important aid for only a minority of institutions, there are signs of a more systematic approach. It seems feasible that the present move to analysis of student needs in terms of course objectives, the increasingly competitive nature of ELT and the need to make the best use of resources in a period of financial stringency, will all eventually contribute to tighter organization and a critical assessment of the role video can play. Under the right conditions, video can begin to fulfil its potential.

THE POTENTIAL AND LIMITATIONS OF VIDEO

DAVE WILLIS

Introduction

All aids, as well as making positive contributions to learning, are potentially dangerous. They can be overused or misused. Video can be overused by a thoughtless programme planner or teacher who harnesses its potential for effective student control rather than effective teaching. Students like video—particularly when it is relatively new to them. It carries an aura of entertainment which can keep students quiet and relatively contented whether they are learning or not. We have all at one time or another sat glassy-eyed through an undemanding TV programme, neither actively enjoying the programme nor summoning the energy to switch it off. Video can be overused in the classroom in exactly the same way. It can be both overused and misused if we require it to do a job which could, with a little forethought, be as well or better done with the help of a simpler aid. It may be used, for example, to present diagrammatic or tabular material which is built up in sequence. The same job may, however, be better done with an overhead projector (OHP) and the careful use of overlays. The OHP has several advantages over video. It offers a bigger, clearer picture. The teacher can more easily point out relevant features of the information displayed. There is better control over the timing of the presentation, which may be particularly important if the information displayed is particularly dense. An OHP skin is in some ways more versatile than a videotape or cassette in that a teacher can choose at the last moment with a given class what information to reveal or conceal, or in what sequence to take the visuals. Finally it is possible to annotate an OHP skin by adding to the original display. If, therefore, teacher control and clarity of picture are of greater importance than a voice-over commentary synchronized with the visuals which can be replayed without variation time and time again, then there may be good arguments for an OHP rather than a video presentation, which may be more effective than video. The purpose of this article is to examine the characteristics of video and see what it can do for us more effectively, conveniently or economically than any other medium of presentation. Given this we can then go on to look at techniques of classroom presentation.

1. Video Compared with Other Aids

Video offers the possibility of showing still or moving pictures in black and white, or, at higher cost, in colour with or without accompanying sound. It is worth comparing the characteristics of video with those of other means of presentation:

1.1 Film

Video has the following advantages over film:

a. It can be used in a normal classroom setting with the room fully lighted.
b. It is quieter in operation than a film projector. There is virtually no extraneous noise.
c. It is simple to stop, start and rewind with a fair degree of accuracy.
d. It has a counter which enables teachers to locate a particular clip. (On most models the counter is less accurate than the counter on an audio player.)
e. The latest models (see Section 2) have a stop-frame facility which can isolate and hold a single picture.
f. A set can conveniently be used by an individual or small group of students for self-study.
g. It is more versatile than film in that material can be:
   i. edited or copied
   ii. copied off-air
   iii. home-produced.

(It should be noted that copying off-air is likely to be an infringement of copyright. This may not be the case with, for example, educational broadcasts in certain countries.)

There are however, certain disadvantages:

a. The picture is smaller and less well defined.
b. The quality of copies and home-produced material may not be ideal. This could be a serious disadvantage with students who are used to television programmes with sound and vision of the highest professional quality.
c. There may be problems of maintenance. These could be severe if video forms are an essential part of a wide range of teaching programmes, particularly if carc is not taken to carry an adequate supply of spare parts and spare equipment.
d. A video capacity is costly to set up and maintain. This is particularly the case if one opts for a production capacity. Home production is time-consuming and some of the costs, for example the time spent by teachers taking part in the programmes may be concealed.
e. Relatively few programmes have been commercially produced specifically for video. This is a disadvantage which may well disappear as video becomes more widely used in the classroom. In the meantime you may be obliged to show in black and white on a small screen a programme that was designed for colour for a much larger screen. Is it still viable?
f. The very advantages of video with its versatile stop–start, rewind and stop-frame facilities make it more demanding on the teacher. A teacher

who is not trained to exploit these facilities may simply be combining the disadvantages of both film and video. There is an obvious need for teacher training and for detailed teaching notes to accompany programmes.

1.2 Tape-Slide/Tape + Teacher Commentary

The obvious difference here is that video offers moving pictures. Given the right slide projection equipment, with remote control and a daylight screen this advantage, although considerable, is the only one. For some teaching purposes a tape-slide presentation may be more effective, since it offers better visuals and better teacher control over the timing of the presentation.

1.3 Micro-Fiche Reader with Synchronized Tape Commentary

This is a relatively new system. The reader/viewer costs about £800, a programme master about £40 and copies of a programme as little as 50p. In the classroom it offers little more than a tape-slide presentation, except that the synchronized recording on the one hand leaves the teacher free and on the other hand means that the presentation is pre-programmed. The microfiche reader has obvious applications for programmed or self-access learning materials.

1.4 OHP

The relative advantages of video and OHP are discussed in the introduction to this article.

1.5 Audio-Tape or Cassette

Depending on the nature and aims of the teaching material, the visual element may distract students' attention from the observation of language. It may, if carelessly used, be over-supportive, so that students respond to the visual message and ignore the spoken word. An active decision must be taken as to whether or not the visual element is a positive aid to learning.

1.6 Video in Conjunction with Other Aids

We are used to exploiting audio-visual aids in harness with one another. An audio presentation may be preceded, followed or accompanied by supporting visuals on OHP, slides or flashcards. The same applies to video. Its use should not be considered in isolation. It is often useful, for example, to have an audio version of a video sound-track, edited if necessary, to provide an opportunity for more detailed linguistic study without visual distraction. In the same way a problem may be presented using video and later discussed in more detail using OHP or slide support.

2. The Visual Element in Communication

We should consider how the visible context supports or modifies our production or comprehension of a verbal message. This can be discussed under four headings—contextualized reference, information weighting, the attitudes of participants in the discourse and, finally, the structuring of the discourse.

2.1 Contextualized Reference

When writing or speaking, we assume a body of shared knowledge. Part of this shared knowledge is derived from a common visual context. It is impossible to assign any value at all to the words *What's it like?* if they are taken out of context. Likewise the words *It's cold* could refer to the weather, the soup, the water in the swimming-pool or any other number of possible referents. In preparing audio materials we are careful to contextualize language by an introduction to the tape or by the use of sound effects or both:

> John and Mary are at the swimming pool. John dives in first. (Splash)
> *Mary*: What's it like?
> *John*: Brrr! It's cold.

There are at least two problems with this kind of presentation:

a. The introduction may be more complex linguistically than the material presented. Either students will be confused or a good deal of time will be spent setting the scene, time which might be used more valuably in contributing more precisely to the aims of the lesson.
b. Given a much longer stretch of language than the example quoted above, either the introduction must be very involved and may, incidentally, make the language which follows largely redundant, or we must, in the audio recording, use language which is more referentially explicit than the language we normally use. If we wish to present a dialogue modelling instructions in the use of a relatively simple piece of equipment, for example, then the language used while demonstrating the use will be quite different from the language used without the visual support of a demonstration.

Both these disadvantages can and should be minimized by the use of static visuals if video is not available. Indeed it may be that supplementary visuals or realia are better suited to some teaching purposes for reasons outlined in Section 1. It is not difficult, however, to think of teaching tasks which can be much better and more economically accomplished with the use of video.

2.2 Information Weighting

We use both verbal and non-verbal devices to emphasize certain aspects of a message. Paralinguistic features, particularly movements of the head and hands, are commonly used to indicate the importance attached to a particular utterance or part of an utterance. Non-verbal devices such as blackboard jottings and diagrams share the joint function of creating an appropriate visual environment and highlighting certain parts of the message.

2.3 *Attitude*

Grammatical and phonological markers of attitude may be reinforced or even replaced by gesture and facial expression. The question *What's it like*? could be answered by a shrug, a grimace, a knowing wink, thumbs up etc. There is a danger that in the absence of visual clues aspects of communication like information weighting and attitude may be missed or we may, as materials producers, compensate for the lack of visual clues by making the spoken message more verbally explicit than necessary or by deliberately exaggerating stress and intonation.

2.4 *Discourse Structure*

Gesture is commonly used to mark or reinforce transitions in discourse. After a few introductory remarks a lecturer, for example, may introduce his topic with the word *Now* . . . accompanied by a stab of his index finger. Again, in a lecture, words used to check on the readiness of students to proceed to the next stage of an argument, such as *OK?*, *Right?*, may be accompanied by a slight raising of the head and eyebrows. Other devices are sometimes used to indicate the value of utterances. Items which are listed and therefore regarded as equivalent in value and status may be counted on the fingers, a proposition which is negative in import may be marked by a shake of the index finger. This kind of visual support is used not only in a lecture but also in everyday exchanges. Turn-taking in English is assisted by eye-contact and body posture, and in an exchange both speaker and listener constantly monitor what is being said with nods of the head, smiles, frowns and so on.

These are all ways in which the visual contributes immediately and directly to communication. There are also aspects of cultural familiarization which can be made easier by a visual presentation. The fact, for example, that customers at a bank in England queue at a counter instead of taking a numbered token, that it is customary in a bar to pay for each drink as it is ordered and that the atmosphere at a University seminar in Britain is relatively informal—all these and other aspects of social behaviour may be relevant to a student who intends to visit Britain or study there.

3. Possible Uses—Towards an Initial Classification

So far we have looked briefly at the potential of video and the part played by the visual element in communication. Before attempting to bring these threads together and consider the possible uses of video in the classroom it is important to look at two distinctions to see how the role of the *native speaker* as a *participant* in an exchange differs from the role of the *learner* as an *observer* of the exchange.

3.1 Participant v Observer

By a participant in an exchange I do not necessarily mean a speaker. A student taking notes at a lecture is a participant. Perhaps the crucial difference between a participant and an observer is that the participant has a 'contextualized agenda'. In an interaction in which participants operate both as addresser and addressee, let us say in an exchange involving a tourist eliciting information from a travel agent, the participants have a more or less precise agenda. The tourist wants, perhaps, to book a holiday for himself, his wife and two children in a warm climate with good bathing facilities for two weeks in the month of July at a total cost of not more than £1,000. His agenda is contextualized by his general knowledge of the world. He knows, perhaps, that the Costa Brava is very crowded in July and that a return charter fare to Barcelona should cost not more than £70. It is contextualized further by his knowledge of and attitude towards more specific circumstances – his wife will accept a self-catering holiday only if there is a maid to do the cleaning and laundry; one of his children is a non-swimmer. The difference between these two kinds of knowledge is that the tourist will assume that the travel agent, too, possesses knowledge of the first kind. The travel agent also has an agenda. Presumably in his case it has something to do with the maximization of profit, but it may be more specific if, for example, he has just had a last minute cancellation which he is anxious to fill. These agendas and the context in which they occur go a long way towards determining the content of an exchange. Most of this information is not initially available to an observer.

Even a participant who functions only as addressee has a contextualized agenda. The university student attends a lecture as part of his course; it is contextualized as part of a larger unit. The student has some idea of the kind of information he will get from the lecture, possibly even a number of specific questions to which he hopes to find answers. He may have a good idea of the lecturer's attitude to the topic. Only a relatively small part of the information put across will actually be new to him, since it is the job of a lecturer to contextualize new information by relating it to his audience's previous experience and learning. It is the student's job to identify and extract what is new and relevant and apply it to his purpose. What all this means is that although video can give us samples of communication it cannot of itself bridge the gap between participant and observer. The language learner is usually in the role of observer.

3.2 *Native-Speaker v Foreign Learner*

A number of factors determine the participants' reliance on the visual element in a message. Most of these, for example the degree of interference with either the oral or the visual element, apply equally to the native speaker and the language learner. There is, however, one important difference. When native speakers communicate with one another each assumes that the other has a considerable means of control over the language code. For everyday purposes we would assume complete control. The message including the visual element is constructed on this premise. The learner, on the other hand, is a learner precisely because he does not have control over language code. He may, therefore, be more reliant on the visual element and may require a much richer visual input if he is to communicate. In the preparation and presentation of teaching material this may lead us into the sort of dangers referred to earlier. We may be over-explicit in visual terms and thus render the spoken message redundant. How far we should rely on the visual will depend on our teaching aims and on how the visual input is developed as part of the teaching process.

On the one hand we have to compensate for the fact that the observer/learner is at a serious disadvantage communicatively compared with the native-speaker/participant. On the other hand we must recognize that our goal is to move the student from the observer/learner role towards the native-speaker/participant role. We may exploit the medium of video by presenting material that is supportive in that it is visually explicit and renders the verbal element to some extent redundant, but we can justify this only insofar as we develop the video presentation in such a way as to make the students less dependent on a visually explicit presentation. A good example of this supportive role of video might occur at the presentation stage of a teaching unit. Here we wish to present language samples the form, meaning or use of which is unfamiliar to the students. The purpose of the video programme is to present a context in which the student can, as observer, infer for himself what he needs to know about the language. Once we have used a video sequence to provide this inferential support we can go on to practise what has been exemplified.

At the other extreme we might use video to present not language items but a target activity. Thus we might make an authentic video of a lecture for intensive study. In this case we could not provide the students with support by making the video programme more visually explicit than it would be in real life, or by selecting a lecture specifically on the grounds that it gave exceptionally good visual support. The supportive material would take the form of supplementary reading, word-lists and so on, to be used at an appropriate stage in the teaching. The justification for the use of video here would be that it enabled students to recognize and take advantage of the visual signals intrinsic to the authentic communication task.

Each of the examples given above implies intensive study of at least part of the verbal and non-verbal aspects of communication actually treated in the video sequence. It is also possible to present information as input to a later language activity which does not necessarily focus on the techniques of communication exemplified in the video. A silent video sequence might be shown to set up a narrative writing exercise or role-play. A programme may be shown in order to promote discussion. In each of these cases the video is intended not to present a sample of communicative activity but to define an activity which is to follow.

Another basic use of video is for socio-cultural orientation. Here again there would be no intensive study of the linguistic or paralinguistic features of the video programme. The function of the programme would be to build up the students' confidence and familiarity with the physical and psychosocial aspects of a foreign language environment. In fact one might easily justify the use of a video programme with commentary in the native rather than the target language.

We can summarize the uses of video outlined so far as follows:

A. Language presentation

Aim: Contextualization of new language items to aid student inference and acquisition.

Video input: Presentation of material in which the visual content compensates for the learner's deficiencies in language code. This can be achieved either by producing a programme which is designed to be visually explicit, or by selecting 'authentic' material which is intrinsically visually explicit.

Examples:

a. Presentation of present perfect used for a past action with present relevance: *Someone has broken the window/I've lost my key* etc. The present perfect rather than the past simple is selected because either the results or the consequences of the past action are visible. The use of camera shots focusing on the results or consequences simultaneously with the use of the appropriate tense form can illustrate this quite clearly. This use of video would be artificially supportive in that the students' attention would be *directed* to visual clues present in the immediate environment.
b. Presentation within a functionally-based syllabus of requests in a shopping situation followed by the fulfilment or refusal of the request. In this case a good many visual clues are intrinsic to the situation. One would anticipate that a customer in a shop is there to request objects of different kinds. Whether these requests are fulfilled or not is also visibly apparent. In this case the video could be 'authentic', although scripted to include the required exponents of the functions to be taught, or it

could be artificially supportive, again by using camera shots to focus students' attention on relevant visual input.

Pre-teaching: Before being asked to identify the target items students should be given enough information to compensate for the observer/participant gap. This might be done through a preliminary showing of the video after which students are asked to identify agenda in broad terms, or it might be done by a teacher introduction either spoken or written. It may be necessary to provide some language input also to provide students with a satisfactory context for inference. This language input should not include an exposition of the items to be taught. It may, however, be worthwhile asking focus questions to aid inference.

Follow-up: The aim of the video is purely presentation. It must therefore be followed by practice in the form of the new items and a production stage in which students are required to use the newly acquired items. The production stage could well be preceded by a showing of the presentation video.

B. Definition of subsequent language task

Aim: To provide information input for a language task.

Examples:

a. A silent video sequence as a preliminary to a role-playing exercise. (This would be the function of the review of the presentation video before the production stage as suggested above.)
b. A video sequence as a preliminary to a narrative writing exercise.

Pre-teaching: It would be necessary before showing the video to give an outline of the task to follow. Again it may be necessary to offer an introduction focusing on specific aspects of the video of particular relevance to the subsequent task.

Follow-up: The video sequence here is preliminary to a specified language activity.

C. Presentation of authentic language activity

Aim: To provide an authentic sample of language use of which the visual element is an essential part.

Examples:

a. A demonstration or experiment;
b. A lecture with supporting graphics.

Pre-teaching: Contextualization for the learner/observer, including focus questions.

Follow-up: Intensive study of the video programme and/or an audio soundtrack or transcript. This could be followed by a parallel task on video.

D. Socio-cultural background

Aim: To build confidence and familiarity with the target environment.

Examples:

a. A guided tour of the university campus on which ESP students will eventually find themselves studying.
b. A sample of social behaviour (e.g. in the restaurant; a formal dinner).

Pre-teaching: Explication, possibly in the native language.

Follow-up: Informal discussion and possibly role-play of a supportive rather than an intensive nature.

This classification represents no more than a broad categorization of the uses of video, and the categories are not intended to be exclusive. Part of a video sequence used for socio-cultural background could be used subsequently, with a quite different treatment, for presentation. The type of video selected, and its exploitation will vary according to the four categories. In categories A and C the video programme itself may be treated intensively. Categories B and D are most unlikely to be treated in this way. In general, as with audio material, the length of a programme will vary inversely with the intensity of study. For presentation at the elementary level a sequence of one or two minutes will provide a good deal of material, and a much longer sequence is likely to be counter-productive. A programme leading in to discussion at the advanced level might usefully be as long as half an hour.

4. The Treatment of Paralinguistics

While paralinguistic features certainly aid communication between native speakers, and often form an essential part of communication and must therefore be in some way systematic, it is extremely difficult to describe such a system. Gesture, in particular, is very idiosyncratic. The possible import of a raised index finger is so varied according to the context and the communicative style of the utterer that it would be impossible to frame any 'rules' for interpretation, and perhaps dangerous even to try. It is not known how far paralinguistic features are cross-cultural. One would guess, however, that different language communities use broadly similar facial expressions. Deictic gestures are also likely to be common. There is probably a greater degree of idiosyncrasy in paralinguistic markers of discourse structure, but even here there is perhaps enough similarity to provide the foreign learner with some clues once his attention has been drawn to such techniques. Paralinguistics are best treated as aids to comprehension with a heavy reliance on carry-over from the native language rather than 'taught' as aspects of behaviour.

THE ROLE OF THE VISUAL ELEMENT IN SPOKEN DISCOURSE: IMPLICATIONS FOR THE EXPLOITATION OF VIDEO IN THE EFL CLASSROOM

JANE WILLIS

Introduction

Non-native speakers of any language are likely to rely more heavily on visual clues to support their comprehension than are native speakers, yet few language course-books deal more than fleetingly with the interpretation of visual elements, e.g. non-vocal communication and importance of setting. This, I presume, is partly due to the fact that research into these areas is at a 'pre-theoretical' stage (Gosling, 1981) and as yet, despite the many and diverse descriptions of particular kinesic features by the ethnomethodologists in the USA, we have no analogous proven system to sentence grammar for analysing and accounting for these visual elements in such a way as to allow us to draw up a teachable pedagogic scheme. So how can we 'teach' students to interpret visual clues more efficiently? And what do we mean by 'teaching'? Perhaps, at one extreme, it is merely a question of *sensitizing* students to what they already recognize at a subconscious level, in their own language and culture, so that they become more efficient at using these clues when interacting in the target language. At the other extreme, as may be the case with students from the Far East, for example, it could be a question of getting them to learn, i.e. *teaching* them, to interpret and respond to a different set of visual clues, settings and non-vocal behaviour from that to which they are accustomed. Unfortunately, studies of 'comparative kinesics' are few and far between, and we know very little about how students from different cultures interpret different visual clues, although research like that of Jim Potts (1978) does help.

Video is an obvious medium for helping students to interpret visual clues effectively and I want, in this paper, to try to draw together the research that has already been carried out which relates to visual elements concerned with interaction. I shall therefore be drawing heavily on the work of many researchers, and in particular that of Riley and his colleagues, which is the only other work (at present) known to me that links the two fields—of video use in ELT and the visual elements of communication—in a practical way. Riley's paper, aptly entitled 'Viewing Comprehension: L'oeil écoute', appears in ELT Documents 1981 Special Issue *The teaching of listening comprehension*. My aim in writing this paper is to build a basis for a set of guidelines for the exploitation of the visual component of video in a more systematic way than has hitherto been achieved in the language classroom.

1. Current Opinions About Video

It appears that it is precisely because of the moving visual component that video is a popular aid in the language classroom, at least with teachers trained in its use. MacKnight's research reveals that teachers like video because they believe it motivates students, bringing real life into the classroom, contextualizing language naturally, 'enabling students to experience authentic language in a controlled environment' (MacKnight, 1981). These beliefs have been borne out by research done into BBC TV Foreign Language Programmes, (Prescott-Thomas, 1980).

Most language students say they find video tape easier to understand than audio tape; Sturtridge (1976) found through informal experimentation that her students preferred a bad quality video tape to a good quality audio tape. It is however dangerous to draw conclusions from subjective comments and informal experiments such as these, because the variables involved are complex and too numerous to handle. Factors like production techniques, style and content of programme, teaching style and teacher expectations, students' backgrounds and previous knowledge can also affect attitudes and preferences for audio or video tape. It is, however, generally accepted that, both in real life and when watching video, being able to see the setting and the speaker helps comprehension and retention and enhances interaction which leads to better communication. It is worth investigating why this is the case.

2. What are the 'Visual Elements'?

I want, in this section, to look more closely at what is meant by 'visual element'. As Holec (1975) points out, it is not just the visual element, but the 'network of interactions between the verbal and non-verbal components' that leads to full comprehension. Although this paper is concerned mainly with non-vocal components, we must remember that both do interrelate most of the time.

2.1 Aural Channel

First of all, however, I want to look at what happens if only the aural channel is used, without the visual, and vice versa. Then we may more easily appreciate the usual interrelations between them. In situations where the visual element is completely lacking, for example, in telephone conversations and radio broadcasts, the aural element becomes more explicit to make up for it. An obvious example is that on the telephone one announces oneself, *Hello. Jane speaking*. Explaining things like street directions on the phone is much harder; there is no shared deictic environment. Interestingly enough, as Morris (1978) points out, people still make gestures when speaking on the phone although they cannot be seen, which shows how automatic such body language is. With radio programmes, there is also a need to be more explicit verbally. In a radio play, a script writer would make sure that when, for example, a parcel or birthday present is unwrapped, the recipient expresses admiration (or otherwise) in such a way as to identify the contents clearly to the listener. Thus, 'the vocal component carries a higher load, the message becomes more explicit, but only in purely vocal terms' (Riley, 1979). The same is often true of language laboratory tapes; to make up for the absence of the visual channel, audio tapes tend to use more verbally explicit language than is usual in real life. Firstly, the settings must be described and the participants identified verbally, for example, the person presenting the drill says:

It's ten o'clock and you're in Tiger's office. His secretary's speaking to you.

(This and later examples are taken from *Kernel Lessons Intermediate Lab Drills, Tapescript*, Longman 1971).

Now, this is perfectly natural English for a stage director, or a classroom teacher setting up a role-play activity, or a language laboratory tape presenter; but would be rarely used in any other circumstances. Secondly, the utterances made by the participants are sometimes over-explicit. If one was standing with a friend, outside the cinema at seven o'clock checking the programme times, one would hardly say *The cinema isn't going to open until eight o'clock*. One would more likely use the pronoun: *It* . . . Similarly, a waiter helping a head waiter to prepare a room for a party, and who has already brought in two lots of flowers, would hardly announce to the head waiter who is standing watching the proceedings in the middle of the room:

I have some more flowers here. What shall I do with them?

The head waiter can, after all, see the flowers, and this *is* the third time; the waiter would be more likely to say simply, *And what about these* or *And where can these go?* He does not need to be more vocally explicit. The danger is, of course, that students get used to more than usually explicit language and find real life interaction very difficult to cope with, being less explicit. Video, of course, does not have this disadvantage because the context is visible and does not have to be described or referred to explicitly. Words like 'these' are disambiguated by use of gesture, direction of gaze, or by the shared knowledge of the setting.

2.2 *Visual Channel*

Let us consider the other extreme, the purely visual channel where aural communication is for some reason impossible. There are, of course, accepted systems of gesture, as in TV studios, and independent sign languages, like the

Tic-tac men on the race course, but these could be considered almost true 'languages' in their own right. Mime artistes are masters of the purely visual channel, but even in everyday life, ordinary people can and often do communicate messages adequately through a purely visual channel. Once attention is gained, normally establishment of eye contact, a variety of messages can be conveyed by facial expression and/or gesture. Imagine two students, **A** and **B**, sitting on different sides of a lecture hall: **A** makes eye contact with **B**, looks at his watch, then aside at the lecturer, raises his eyebrows, then looks at the door, then at **B**, who engages eye contact, shrugs, and starts packing up his books. This message will probably have conveyed: **A**–*It's late, I'm bored, isn't it time he stopped? Shall we go, anyway?* **B**–*Suppose so. OK then. Let's go*. In fact, quite a complex piece of communication has taken place, non-vocally. A similar interaction has in fact been recorded by Gosling (1981).

2.3 Interrelations Between Aural and Visual Elements

Normally, the interrelations between the aural and visual elements are somewhere along the clinc between these two extremes, and the one is dependent, to varying degrees, upon the other. In real life, they usually supplement each other; in the language classroom, however, the visual is often used to duplicate the aural channel in order to 'clarify' meaning of a new language item, or to prompt a student, as with the 'Audio-Visual' approach of the 1960s (ref. Widdowson, 1980, who has illustrated this). The danger is obvious: the student rarely gets practice in interpreting and recognizing visual clues as they are used in real life, to supplement rather than duplicate the message being conveyed. As Riley (1979) points out, 'This semiotic relationship–parallel coding of the same message–is totally different from the integrated and cumulative role played by non-vocal features in face-to-face interaction, where they converge to contribute to a final meaning or message of which they are an intrinsic part.' Thus an awareness of the possible real life interrelations between visual and aural channels is vital for the language teacher. Perhaps one way of experiencing more acutely the interrelations between the aural and visual channels is to imagine oneself talking to an unknown blind person in an unfamiliar setting. One quickly realizes in what ways one needs to compensate for the other's lack of sight in order to communicate efficiently. An alternative way would be to listen to stretches of a TV film without watching, or indeed having seen, the picture on the screen, thus putting oneself into the position of a blind person, remembering though that even TV scripts tend to err on the side of being over-explicit verbally.

2.4 Components of the Visual Element

Before we begin to judge to what extent the visual element affects communication in general, and language teaching in particular, we need to define more precisely what the visual element consists of.

2.4.1 To start with, the distinction must somehow be made between the visual elements that affect the message, and those that do not. Let us consider the physical setting, which may or may not be part of the message. MacKnight (1981) points out 'There may be little correlation, or even a mismatch, between audio and visual elements, e.g. two women child-minding and discussing a concert.' Hutchinson and Waters (1980), on the other hand, show that technical instruction is usually visually dependent. How, other than by relating to the visual elements (here a workshop) could one understand the instruction, 'You just shove this little chappie in here like that?'

Against the visual background of the physical setting, we have the participants interacting. How much significance does dress, for example, have? How much meaning is lost if a non-native speaker fails to recognize a particular uniform or the significance of a pin-striped suit and a rolled umbrella? What can these, in conjunction with the setting, tell us about the status of the participants and the type of interaction to anticipate? How do we learn to distinguish idiosyncratic gestures or nervous tics from significant message-bearing movements? How much of a psychological effect can they have, e.g. on the establishment of rapport, even if such movements are not concerned with conveying the intended message? As language teachers, we must not only distinguish the visual aspects which form part of the message, but also which visual features are vital to non-vocal communication and again, which of these are in fact teachable and indeed worth teaching? This is summarized in Figure 1 below.

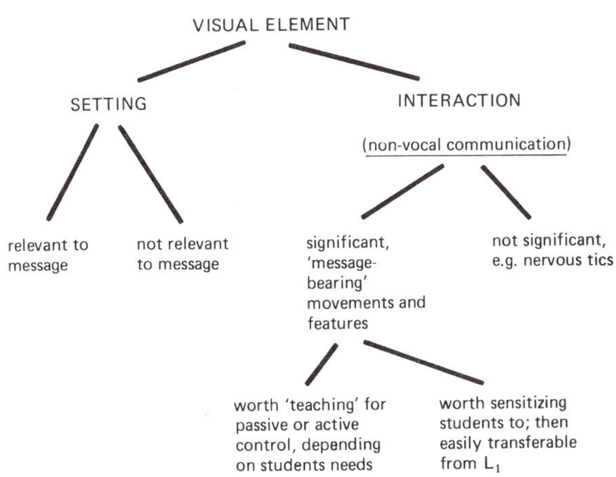

Figure 1

2.4.2 Next, we need to break down non-vocal communication into more specific features. As I have already stated, in the introduction to this paper, there have been many studies of non-vocal behaviour, and although they differ in depth, extent, and terminology, they also overlap in many areas. For the purposes of this paper, I have chosen the simplest and yet most finite set of categories, which in fact cover most features reported by other researchers, those proposed by Abercrombie (1968) in his paper on *Paralanguage*. (I am fully aware that more recent research has explored deeper into some areas since 1968, but as a set of categories they are still useful because they are finite.) Abercrombie states that 'paralinguistic activities must (a) communicate and (b) be part of a conversational interaction.' He also distinguishes between elements that can stand independently of conversation, e.g. a nod for yes (non-vocal surrogates) and those which must be dependent on conversation, e.g. a hand gesture to indicate emphasis. He lists the following categories for visible paralinguistic elements:

posture	the general way the whole body is disposed, either when sitting or standing during conversation
proxemics	the distance at which people naturally stand from each other in various circumstances
gesture	superimposed on posture, involves less of the body at any one time, and changes more rapidly
facial expression	
eye contacts	

Some of these can be either dependent or independent of conversation, like gesture and facial expression; others, like posture and postural change, are usually dependent on conversation for the communication to be significant. Apart from some kinds of gesture and facial expression which may be idiosyncratic, it has been shown that the visible elements listed above are not used randomly: some fulfil specific discourse functions, e.g. preparing the ground to interrupt the speaker: for others there seem to be unwritten rules for their use, which may vary to some extent across cultures.

On *posture*, Abercrombie reports that Scheflen (1964) found that 'changes in posture have a punctuative role in conversation; they indicate the beginnings and endings of contributions to the interaction, show when a point has been made . . .' This has been borne out consistently by more recent research, including that of Mehan *et al.* (1976) and Gosling (1981), who have found a high correlation between particular postural shifts and beginnings and endings of vocal transactions.

Research has shown, for example, that a seated lecturer is likely to lean forward when beginning a vital explanation, and then lean back when the explanation is over, when he is ready to continue with another topic. In other words, he may shift his position slightly to mark the 'boundary'. A student wanting to speak in a seminar will first orientate himself towards the seminar leader in a first step towards gaining speaker's rights.

Posture can certainly give some indication of participants' attitudes both towards each other and to what is being said. Different postures can express solidarity and agreement between speakers, or challenge; as well as willingness or otherwise to participate in a conversation. If you do not want to speak to your fellow passenger on a Boeing 747 you may well turn your shoulder and/or cross your legs away from your neighbour, forming a 'closed' position . . . I would also imagine that posture of different types could denote status; in some cultures, 'humble' and 'superior' beings have characteristic postural styles.

Proxemics also vary across cultures, and there is much evidence, both anecdotal and researched (Hall, 1964; Morris, 1978) to show that misunderstanding can be caused by general lack of sensitivity to cultural differences in the concept of one's 'private space'. French businessmen put English businessmen on the defensive by standing too close; South Americans are considered too familiar for the same reason, and English people are 'cold and distant'. (Morris, 1978).

Eye contact is used differently in the East; some Moslem women, for example, are not expected to make eye contact with people outside their immediate family: how do they then manage to begin a conversation in UK, where eye contact is a necessary pre-condition for doing so? (Gosling, 1981).

Uses of gesture include deictic reference, as in *Shall I put these over there?* and giving attitudinal information, as in the dismissive hand and arm gesture that could accompany *Oh never mind, forget it!* Gestures also fulfil a more purely linguistic function, and this function can usefully be divided into the four categories suggested by Riley (1979):

(a) Emblems (verbal surrogates, e.g. a 'V sign')
(b) Illustrators (e.g. gesture to match, *It was this shape*)
(c) Enactions (beckoning to command *Come here*)
(d) 'Batons' (hand or head movements related to stress, rhythm and tempo)

Of these categories, 'emblems' and 'enactions' may well differ from culture to culture. The Greek and Middle Eastern backward tilt of the head for 'no' can easily be mistaken by a Westerner for a nod meaning 'yes'; the thumbs-up sign, acceptable in UK, is extremely offensive in the Middle East. However, it is not these one-off, possibly anti-social, gestures that are likely to cause miscommunication; these are, like lexical items, easily taught and easily learnt (or avoided!) It is the other features, for example, proxemics and eye contact, which consistently come into play and could affect continuous whole episodes of interaction, interfering with the establishment of rapport, even to the point of offending people. How far these can be actually taught depends on a whole range of psycho- and socio-linguistic elements. Some students may find it much harder to break a taboo than to learn the past tense of common irregular verbs.

Facial expression conveys attitudinal (or 'affective') information both to the hearer, who watches the speaker's face to judge to what extent he is committed to the literal meaning of what he is saying, and also to the speaker, who watches the hearer's face for feedback, in other words, to monitor the effect his words are having on the hearer. Gesture and postural shift also give attitudinal information, as do other features such as intonation, stress, voice intensity and choice of modal verb, but, to the Westerner, lack of facial expression, especially in the hearer, can lead to communication breakdown. In the Far East where one is not supposed to show one's true feelings, facial expression carries less information, which Westerners can find worrying. (Hence the term 'inscrutable' applied to Chinese speakers.)

So far we have examined the relationship between the aural and visual channels, and looked at the relative importance of the physical setting, the appearance of the participants, and at specific features of non-vocal communication. Figure 2 begins to set these out in a more systematic way.

3. Interpretation of the Visual Elements

3.1 Exploitation of Visual Sequences

Effective and systematic exploitation of well-selected video sequences could help to sensitize students to vital differences in non-vocal communication, as well as serve as a stimulus for free discussion in English. To do this, though, the teacher needs to have a clear idea of what visual features there are that can be exploited, and of the possible interrelations between these and the aural channel, i.e. vocal communication. In Figure 2 I have tried to display systematically what these visual features are and describe what types of information they can give.

To interpret Figure 2 more easily, imagine yourself as you begin viewing an unfamiliar TV or video programme with the volume switches OFF; you will then be nearer the position (but not in the same position, for *you* will

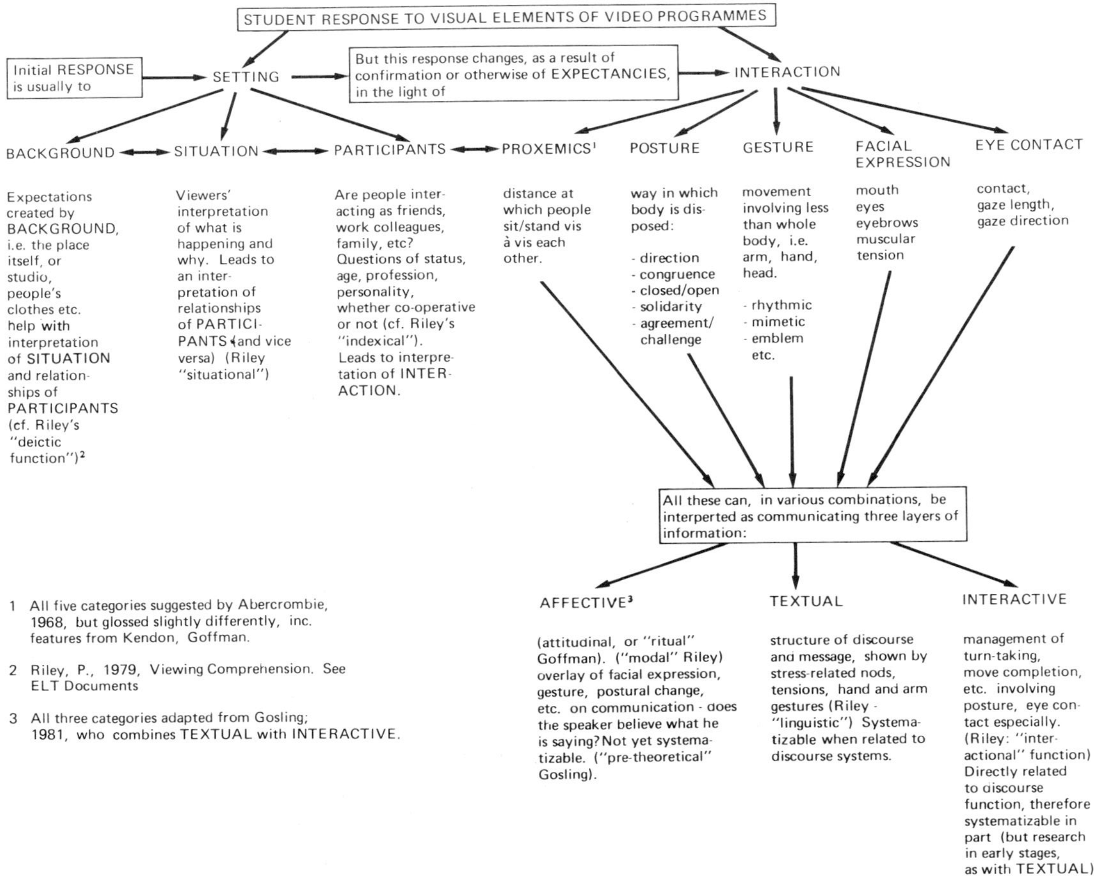

Figure 2

1 All five categories suggested by Abercrombie, 1968, but glossed slightly differently, inc. features from Kendon, Goffman.

2 Riley, P., 1979, Viewing Comprehension. See ELT Documents

3 All three categories adapted from Gosling; 1981, who combines TEXTUAL with INTERACTIVE.

understand the significance of various visual elements more clearly) of the non-native speaker with very little English.

It is important, however, to remember that the effects of background music (suspenseful, eerie, triumphant), people's intonation patterns, pace, voice volume and intensity may also change the viewer's expectation and subsequent interpretation of SETTING and INTERACTION initially as much, if not more, than the verbal message itself.

Although Figure 2 attempts to draw together the various visual elements as identified and described by various researchers, it should be regarded as a basis for a pedagogic model rather than a serious attempt to provide a theoretical model. Each element will carry a different weighting in the classroom depending, for example, upon the video content and the needs and cultural backgrounds of the students. Not all programmes will lend themselves to the exploitation of all elements, and not all students will find the same elements problematic.

3.1.1 I will look more closely at the *layers of information* conveyed by the visual components, as summarized in Figure 2, on the right at the bottom.

As we have touched on earlier, not all kinesic features are yet systematized or systematizable; those communicating AFFECTIVE information, for example, are not, and these can be a combination of vocal and non-vocal features, for example, use of modals, intonation, gesture, posture and facial expression. But as Riley points out, 'by asking students questions like "Is A teasing B?" "Is A being sarcastic (ironic, formal, aggressive, hypothetical, etc.)?" the teacher goes directly to the heart of the matter: there is little point in waiting until we have, say, an integrated theory of the meaning of facial expression before asking ourselves why A smiles at a given moment!' To understand whether a supervisor who, having read an assignment, comments *Mm. You've said quite a lot about area x* is expressing disquiet or pleasure, one would probably need to fall back upon non-verbal evidence. It is, from my experience, extremely difficult to judge attitude in a foreign language, especially when one's attention is focused narrowly on the verbal message; one often disregards the visual clues to meaning. Tutors and families who have close contact with foreign learners sometimes find that their words are taken literally, that the function of the utterance is not recognized, as when a comment on a situation is intended as a request. The above example could, for instance, 'mean'—*Cut down that section about area x!* The non-vocal component may hold the vital clue, and this in turn could help the non-native speaker recognize the status of the information they receive as well as the attitude of the speakers or programme producer/presenter. Video can give students practice in inferring attitudes as well as recognizing messages that are implicit in a programme; for example, in the Open University 'case-study' type of programme, where the viewer is required to draw his own conclusions about the intended message from the way the evidence is selected, assembled and given. Appreciation of signals of attitude is vital, too, if a student is to establish rapport with a peer group and make friends in a foreign country. Inability to do this often causes embarrassment and awkwardness in personal relations, but this needs to be a two-way process, the native speaker also being aware of the difficulties and making allowances. Short recordings (again unedited) in informal peer-group situations would be useful, if it were possible for participants to sustain such informal interaction naturally while knowing they were being recorded. Other materials, like the Video Arts films, are often suitable for these purposes, even though they are scripted and not altogether 'genuine'.

As far as the TEXTUAL layer is concerned, we have evidence that the rhythmic hand and arm movements, head nods, hand gestures, etc. are directly related to the structure of the message, and therefore to some extend systematizable. If you have ever watched a monologue on film where the sound and vision were not synchronized at all, you will have found it very difficult to understand. Some years ago, the BBC once began showing a short piece of film clandestinely filmed in Czechoslovakia; due to difficult recording circumstances and technical problems the sound was about 10–15 seconds ahead of the vision. The only way to understand the speaker was to close your eyes. It proved, however, so impossible to *watch* with understanding that the BBC apologetically took it off the air before it had finished, despite the fact that the verbal message was itself quite explicit and the film itself of great interest to viewers. We know that head nods and baton movements coincide with the tonic or stressed syllables, and that different size and type of head movements as well as postural shifts often mark 'boundary' exchanges, for example, at the beginning of a new topic (see 2.4.2 on posture for an example). It would be interesting to discover whether TV presenters or lecturers visibly mark their key points in a particular way. Gosling (1981), commenting on delimitation of linguistic transactions, states "much detailed work still remains to be done. However, there does seem to be something of a kinesically-observable relationship to discourse topic, and to the use by participants (particularly by T = the tutor) in this (i.e. seminar) interaction of metadiscoursal terms, like 'point', or 'thing' or 'question', to indicate some kind of conceptual unit in the discourse." Unfortunately he does not exemplify how this happens. Students could in fact help research these areas; for example, they could certainly be asked to view a video recording with the volume off to see if they could distinguish the points in the sequence or section at which the key points are stated. The resulting discussion would also be useful language practice.

The INTERACTIVE layer, which involves the management of the 'address system', e.g. reciprocity and turn-taking behaviour, can be directly related to discourse function. Riley states 'This (interactive) structure and these behaviours are almost exclusively regulated by visually perceived non-vocal communication – gaze, above all, but also posture, orientation and gestures.' Gosling (1981), in his analysis of seminar interaction, has found that in turn-taking procedures, there is a typical pattern of consecutive body movements, building up 'like a pyramid and culminating in eye contact which gives one the right to a turn to speak.' Such address systems, Riley has found, differ tremendously, not only from culture to culture (I have already mentioned the taboo on eye contact in the Middle East) but from setting to setting. Compare classroom interaction, where the teacher controls the right to speak, to family interaction where children are not supposed to interrupt adults, down to informal status-equal neutral-setting casual peer-group conversation. My own research (Willis, 1981) has shown that even casually, in informal ELT classrooms, address systems and interaction patterns are in no way representative of interaction outside the classroom. Perhaps our overseas students, once sensitized to Gosling's analysis of turn-taking in a seminar situation, could actually contribute to the research here, by watching, observing, discussing a video sequence of a seminar discussion, and then performing themselves, being recorded on video tape to note differences and similarities. Understanding the kinesics of turn-taking could certainly help shyer students to 'get in' to a discussion, and become participants rather than purely listeners.

Gosling also found that 'it seems possible to use non-vocal behaviour to maintain a speaking turn (i.e. continue speaking rights) even though in terms of realizations at other levels (syntactic, phonological) the turn should really have come to an end. In other words, people, as part of their socialization, learn to recognize kinesic signals of dominance from others, and react accordingly. Whether these signals are common to all cultures is not yet known, but our students should at least be sensitized to their presence in English interactions. We need, in fact, unedited, unscripted video recordings of a variety of interactions taking place in the settings likely to be experienced by the students concerned, illustrating variations in interactive behaviour due to differences in degrees of formality, types of setting, register, status, group relations and so on. After observing and discussing the address systems illustrated by the video (perhaps viewing with the volume OFF to guess who is going to speak next) students should be given plenty of opportunities to take part in activities that require similar kinds of behaviour, for example, job interviews, various social events, or informal small group 'exploratory' discussions. Also useful, especially for practice in relating language to the physical setting (see 2.4.1) would be video recordings of practical work relevant to students' needs, e.g. laboratory or workshop demonstrations, or of lectures involving references to visual aids, but these should be followed up by practical work in which students themselves participate, in order to gain first-hand experience of the interrelations between aural and visual channels of communication.

4. A Concluding Caveat

There are, however, some points which must be kept in mind by the language teacher.

Video, even unscripted and unedited video, is *not* 'real life'; watching and analysing an interaction on video *is* useful, but students still need to practise doing things for themselves after viewing. As observers, they may gain receptive skills but only as active participants will they gain productive skills. Video is a means to an end, not an end in itself.

The camera, and the TV screen, give a very circumscribed view of a scene. Students do not gain practice in picking up clues from their peripheral vision; the camera view point is always narrower and more limited. Also, with video, the producer has chosen the significant shots for the viewer—in real life students have to select what is important for themselves, their eyes are not automatically guided to the significant details. Often, for language learning, e.g. analysing turn-taking behaviour, one needs a much wider shot of an interaction than the TV producer, trained in the grammar of television is happy to provide; a series of close-ups of speakers in a seminar does not reveal the system of turn-taking that Gosling describes. There is, in fact, a *dichotomy* between television production for language teaching and production of 'good television'. Tony Bates, writing of Open University programmes, says that good educational programmes do not necessarily make 'good television' and vice versa; similarly, with language teaching programmes. If the language teacher can record sequences especially for language teaching, this should not be forgotten. A fixed camera may well be more useful than an expert camera man, for short sequences at least; students should be made aware of the constraints and purposes of such recordings, so as not to be disappointed to find less than expert production. However, the quality of the sound and the picture must be sustained, or the message itself may well be lost.

Conclusion

In order to cover the relevant visual features outlined in this paper, one needs to exploit a wide selection of short video extracts specifically chosen to illustrate the variety of social and work settings and types of interaction needed to widen the students' socio-linguistic experience. It would be impossible to study each visual element as a discrete item, out of context; it is, after all, the network of interrelated aural and visual lines that make up 'communication'.

If students are made aware, in a systematic way, of the existence and comparative importance of the visual elements which we have discussed, they will become far more evaluative viewers, and be far better equipped to continue learning from TV independently of the teacher in the future. Their visual comprehension strategies will have been heightened, and their exposure to a wider variety of settings and interactions via the medium of video, coupled with enactions of similar situations in class in which they themselves take part, will serve to give them a greater measure of confidence outside the classroom.

Notes and References

ABERCROMBIE, A. (1968) 'Paralanguage', in Laver, J. and Hutchinson, S. *Communication in Face to Face Interaction*, Penguin, 1972.

BATES, A. (1981) *Towards a Better Research Framework for Evaluating the Effectiveness of Educational Media*, IET Paper on Broadcasting No. 172, Open University.

GOSLING, J. (1981) 'Kinesics in Discourse' in Coulthard, M. and Montgomery, M. (eds) *Studies in Discourse Analysis*, Routledge Kegan-Paul.

HALL, E. T. (1964) *Silent Assumptions in Social Communication* in Laver, J. and Hutchinson, S. (1972), *op. cit.*

HOLEC, H. (1975) 'L'approche macro-linguistique du fontionnement des langues et ses implications pedagogiques: role du visuel', *Mélanges Pédagogiques du C.R.A.P.E.L.*

HUTCHINSON, T. A. and WATERS, A. (1980) *ESP at the Crossroads*, ESP 36, Oregon State University.

MacKNIGHT, F. (1981) *Review and Analysis of Present Video Use in EFL Teaching*, M.Ed. Thesis, University of Wales (UCC Cardiff).

MEHAN, H., CAZDEN, C. B. *et al.* (1976) *The Social Organisation of Classroom Lessons*, CRIP Report, La Jolla, University of San Diego, California.

MORRIS, D. (1978) *Manwatching*, Triad/Granada.

POTTS, J. (1978) in *Educational Broadcasting International.*

PRESCOTT-THOMAS, J. (1980) 'Close Encounters—of four kinds: the Development of BBC Schools Television Language Broadcasts' in *British Journal of Language Teaching*, **18**, Nos. 2 and 3 combined for Winter 1980.

RILEY, P. (1979) 'Viewing Comprehension "L'oeil ecoute"', *Mélanges Pédagogiques du C.R.A.P.E.L.*, also appears in ELT Documents 1981, Special Issue *The Teaching of Listening Comprehension.*

SCHEFLEN, A. E. (1964) *The Significance of Posture in Communication Systems* in Laver, J. and Hutchinson, S. (1972), *op. cit.*

STURTRIDGE, G., McALPIN, J. and HARPER, D. (1978) 'The British Council and the English language problems of overseas students: English for Academic Purposes materials development' in Cowie and Heaton (eds), *English for Academic Purposes*, BAAL/SELMOUS.

Video Arts Ltd., are the producers of *The Video Arts Training Films in the Fields of Management, Sales and Customer Relations.* Video Arts Ltd., Dumbarton House, 68 Oxford Street, London W1N 9LA.

WIDDOWSON, H. (1980) 'Contrived and Natural Language', *EFL T.A. Bulletin Issue 4*, OUP.

WILLIS, J. (1981) *Spoken Interaction in the EFL Classroom: a system of analysis and a description*, M.A. Thesis, University of Birmingham.

101 WAYS TO USE VIDEO

JANE WILLIS

Introduction

It is comparatively easy for any group of imaginative teachers experienced in using video for ELT to sit down and draw up a list of 101 different ways of using video in the classroom; there are many accounts where interesting 'video lessons' are reported in the literature, and there will be many more. There seems, however, to be a constant danger of lapsing into the anecdotal; 'I did this with my students and it was a great success' does not mean that the same video lesson, i.e. the same video sequence, used in the same way will be equally successful with a different group.

Should we, in fact, be talking about 'video lessons' at all? We do not talk about 'blackboard lessons' or 'textbook lessons'. Video is a teaching aid; video materials can be valuable teaching resources, in the same way as text-books or audio tape recordings; video is not an end in itself. As we have already seen in this volume (Willis, J. D. *The Potential and Limitations of Video*), video merely adds a further dimension—that of moving picture and synchronized sound—to the teaching aids and material formats we already use. It follows, then, that very many teaching techniques and classroom activities we already use in conjunction with other aids and materials can also be used (with minor adaptations to suit the properties of video equipment) with video materials. Since we already use different combinations of aids and materials (e.g. audio tape and blackboard and printed text) we now have even more combinations available with the addition of video, which in turn has its own combinations—picture without sound, sound without picture, etc.

Immediately this opens up a wealth of possibilities for ways to use video materials both on their own and in conjunction with other aids and formats. Some examples will be discussed later in Section 2. However, whichever aid, format or combination of aids is used, the same basic pedagogic and linguistic principles which need to be applied must surely remain.

The problem is that in the excitement of experimenting with a relatively new medium there is a tendency for video users (both us, as teachers, and students themselves) to lose sight of language teaching objectives, and of students' own learning objectives, and to use video for insufficiently motivated purposes. This problem is aggravated by the fact that students are not conditioned to regarding the TV screen as a teaching device to be used selectively, in a similar way to, say, their textbooks. (The problem of 'marketing' video as a teaching tool is discussed later, in Section 2.) The result is often that neither students nor teachers have specific and valid language learning aims in mind once the video has been switched on. The one hundred and one possible ways to use video fade fast from our minds as the television screen begins (in its compelling way) its mesmerization process.[1] Switching off before the end of the programme becomes a decidedly anti-social gesture for us, as teachers, to make.

1. Language Learning Objectives and the Role of Video

In an attempt to explore and classify the uses of video-taped recordings to fulfil specified language objectives and to meet stated student needs, I have drawn up a tentative framework which allows us to establish more clearly the potential roles of video in the ELT classroom. This is now explained.

1.1 Overall View

The framework appears as a chart opposite. It is ultimately intended as a reference document to be read vertically down the columns, thus linking the general language learning objectives in the upper section with the possible roles of video and with examples of suitable activities involving video. Hence, the lower section of the chart which applies specifically to video, needs to be interpreted in the light of the upper section, which outlines language learning objectives in more general terms.

Initially, then, it is a good idea to read across the upper section, where the general language learning OBJECTIVES are outlined in stages, and suggestions made for the UNIT OF TEXT (spoken or written) to be used at each stage. While reading across, bear in mind the implications of the FOCUS SHIFT[2], which indicates the fact that in the early stages of the language learning process the emphasis is more on language forms than in the later stages, where the message conveyed by thc language receives more attention.

1.2 Detailed Guide

The rest of this section is devoted to more detailed explanations of the horizontal categories of the chart, and thus needs to be read in conjunction with the chart itself.

OBJECTIVES

In the upper section of the chart are set out, in five broad stages, the changes that occur in language teaching objectives as a result of increasing language proficiency, both in the short term, as seen over a lesson or series of lessons, and in the long term, as students progress from 'elementary' to 'intermediate' and 'advanced'.[3] These objectives will obviously need to be adapted and

LANGUAGE LEARNING OBJECTIVES AND THE ROLE OF VIDEO

	1	2	3	4	5	
STAGED OBJECTIVES	As a result of controlled exposure to target language, sts. will be able to grasp the general situation and repeat and memorize selected language items in a controlled way in limited contexts; e.g. an Initiating move + Responding move, with perhaps, a follow-up move.	Sts. should be able to recognize wider contexts for using language they have learnt, in fairly controlled, predictable situations; understand other realizations of similar functions; also to initiate/respond, using whatever language they can, with slightly less teacher help.	Students should be able to recognize language items they know in genuine use in wider situations, and begin to transcode information retrieved in a controlled way, guided by Teacher+B/B or print materials; begin to interpret more systematically, features of communication (e.g. non-verbal presented in the context.	Sts. should be able to recognize the overall structure of a text (spoken/written) & begin to produce organized discourse (rather than discrete items) themselves. This involves practice of microskills e.g. recognizing the value of sentences in a text, moves in an interaction, also predicting transcoding (still with guidance).	Sts. should be able to present and retrieve information (factual and inferred), evaluate and respond appropriately, e.g. report, reformulate for a different purpose, discuss, interact efficiently at different levels of formality etc.	
UNIT OF TEXT / SPOKEN UNIT OF TEXT \ WRITTEN	Exchange/ short sequence of exchanges/very short extract from monologue.	Sequence of exchanges/short extract from monologue.	Sequence → transaction Paragraph → series of paragraphs	Transaction → interaction Short text (not necessarily complete)	Interaction (complete but short) Complete text (but not too lengthy)	
FOCUS SHIFT	LANGUAGE →				MESSAGE	
ROLE OF VIDEO	MODEL AND CUE To present new language items in short, well-contextualized situations, illustrating meaning & use; to give listening practice & chance for selective controlled oral practice, possibly in conjunction with audio tape. Also, with Vol. OFF, to provide sequences of visual clues for teacher modelled 'drilling' e.g. practice in these forms.	TARGET To show 'target' situations that sts. can re-enact using their own words. e.g. simple role play, to introduce a wider variety of settings & interactions, related to those used previously but less predictable, extending listening skills, giving sts. practice in recognizing different realisations of similar functions.	TRANSFER & REINFORCEMENT To illustrate target language in use in a far wider variety of relevant situations, using longer episodes, to stimulate simulation to provide material suitable for simple transcoding, under guidance: note-taking with matrix to introduce features of continuous text, e.g. signalling devices, discourse markers.	ILLUSTRATOR of MESSAGE and DISCOURSE STRUCTURE To expose sts. to larger chunks of language that they may not initially understand, but which illustrate typical text structures and allow practice in comprehension skills and strategies.	SOURCE of INFORMATION To provide material of which the content is relevant to sts. needs & interests, for the purpose of information retrieval (activities in real life) to provide and resource material for related oral/ written tasks e.g. simulations presenting a mini-lecture writing a report.	STIMULUS To provide material to act as a stimulus for freer classroom activities (problem solving, games etc) not necessarily based on the intended message of the programme
SEQUENCE LENGTH (see UNIT OF TEXT above)	30 seconds to 2 minutes	1–3 minutes	2–4 minutes	3–5 minutes	3–8 minutes	4–12 minutes
Examples of ACTIVITIES whole class group pairs one abs. for viewing PIC + VOL VOL OFF NO PIC.	-View and → select -View and identify -View and do -View and repeat -Watch and identify -Watch and discuss (? L') -Watch and analyse -Watch and drill -Listen and match with picture/text	-Watch & speculate -Watch & identify -Watch & analyse -Watch & improvize -View and explain to non-viewers -View and report to non-viewers -View and do/ repeat/analyse -View & re-enact -View & complete -View & re-create	-View and identify language/message -View and re-arrange (main points, texts, Qs) -View & write (notes) (Matrix, Cloze/As to Qs) -Watch & provide V/O. -Watch & analyse kinesics. -Watch/view and report. -Listen and speculate about visual content	-Predict from ← title and discuss. -Study related materials and discuss. -View and note-take (guided) -Watch & analyse. 'Jigsaw' viewing + written/audio texts. -Write related tasks.	similar to ← 3 -inc. listen/ watch. -Sts. view then report, evaluate, compare, summarize, combine with info. from other sources; write & record own sound track, role-play related situations.	also → ← discussions of cultural & social customs & values. -Information gap (split viewing) -Plan/replan programme to give different attitudes. -Debate. Write related tasks (e.g. letter to BBC)

made more specific to suit the needs of particular student groups. I have deliberately tried to keep them as general as possible while still being informative.

Considering the five objects from the long-term angle first. OBJECTIVES 1 and 2 pertain to any elementary stage class, 2 and 3 (and sometimes 1) to intermediate, 3–5 to later intermediate and advanced stages. At any stage, however, any of the earlier objectives may have occasional validity, just as, with a remedial class, all five objectives are likely to be valid at different times.

Within each stage, we should be aware of the need to reassess objectives constantly as a result of student achievement over the short term, as each learning cycle comes to completion. Compare, for example, objective 1 with objective 2, or 3 with 4.

UNITS OF TEXT

The terminology used here for the units of spoken text is in accordance with the description of the model for the analysis of spoken interaction developed over the last 12 years at the University of Birmingham and which is now beginning to be applied to the design of teaching materials.[4]

It is generally accepted that the earlier the stage, the shorter the 'unit' of language presented. This is, of course, only a general rule; obviously the length of text will depend on what the student is expected to do with it, e.g. imitate, summarize or merely comprehend specific items. In very early stages, students might be restricted to the production of simple two or three-part exchanges, consisting of an Initiation, a Response and perhaps a Follow-up move. These could either be exchanges that are complete 'interactions' in themselves, for example, two people passing in street might say only:

A Excuse me, do you have the time? (*Initiation*)
B Er yes, it's ten o'clock. (*Response*)
A Thank you. (*Follow-up*)

and then go on their separate ways. Or it could be a chain of identical exchanges, for example, those used when filling out a form for someone else:

A What's your name?
B Rebecca Bloggs.
A What's your address?
B 21 Park Road.
A Telephone number?
B 3612.
A Thanks. That's all.

However, we cannot always find suitable exchanges that are complete interactions in themselves; in which case a single exchange, itself embedded in a short sequence of other exchanges, can be taught for productive control, while the surrounding language which contextualizes the exchange can, if they do not already know it, be taught for receptive control—for aural comprehension, only. An example follows:

(Frances meets Paul in the street)

P Hello, Frances, glad we met. Look, are you free on Friday? Friday evening?
F Yes, I think so, Paul.
P We're having a party. Could you come?
F Oh, yes please. That would be nice. What time?
P About eight.
F Eight o'clock. Right. Oh, by the way, have you seen Fred lately?
P Fred? No, not since . . .

the central exchange being the one taught initially for productive control. The terminology used for the UNITS in the chart is now explained with reference to the above dialogue. The first four exchanges here make up one 'transaction', the 'boundaries' of which are marked by *Look* at the beginning and *Right* at the end. A new 'transaction' then begins, marked by *Oh, by the way* . . . These two (or maybe more) 'transactions' will form the complete 'interaction' which will be the extent of the casual meeting between Frances and Paul. Usually, then, an 'interaction' (which consists of one or more 'transactions') is a longer, more complex unit than a 'transaction', and, in turn, a 'transaction' (made up of a series of 'exchanges') is almost always a longer and more complex unit than an exchange. It is, however, possible to have, as we saw from the first example, a complete interaction made up of one transaction made up of one exchange, but this is rare. So, normally, unless we can find such simple 'complete' interactions, we would wait until the later stages (see objectives 4–5) to introduce a unit of text as long, or complex, as the usual complete interaction (e.g. a whole lecture or a job interview). This has obvious implications for the selection of video sequences as it does for the selection or writing or recording of reading or listening texts; some kind of complete 'unit' is preferable, but the length and complexity of the overall structure of the unit depend on the language teaching objectives.

The commonly used term 'video sequence' seems to suggest some idea of 'completeness' although, as far as I have found, the term 'sequence' is nowhere formally defined. It seems to be used to indicate an extract from a video programme, but the length and complexity of that extract is variable. I suggest that we adopt the term 'sequence' only for an extract that consists of a 'complete unit' as defined above, i.e. either a whole transaction, or a series of exchanges that make some sense on their own. Anything smaller, i.e. less complete, would be termed a 'segment'. 'Chunk' remains a suitable term for a loose, undefined extract, yet to be analysed into units suitable for teaching.

In the chart, I have used the terminology referring to the structure of interactive discourse in order to give a more specific definition of *sequence*, i.e. giving an idea of the length and complexity of the UNIT of language that can be used at each stage to fulfil each objective. Although written language should also be considered interactive, there is no such generally accepted terminology for units of written discourse; hence I have kept to the traditional terms, 'Sentence', 'paragraph' and 'text';[5] but these are more meaningful if seen not as discrete items, but as parts of a whole and in relation to the units of spoken discourse.

FOCUS SHIFT

At very early stages, even if the new language items are well contextualized, and presented and practised in a meaningful way, there is inevitably a very great degree of emphasis on the form of the new language items. As the learning cycle progresses, and as the amount of control imposed by the teacher or the materials decreases, the language used becomes less predictable, and the focus shifts from language as a tool, i.e. lexis, grammar, intra- and inter-sentential relations, and discourse structure, to the message conveyed by the language, i.e. its informational content and its functional use. This is shown diagrammatically in the table as a single cline, which represents an average shift of focus; as students' language proficiency increases, less attention is drawn to the form of specific language items, and more attention paid to comprehension and expression of a message. This focus shift will not normally be as steady as the straight cline suggests. Recent research has shown that in the language classroom the focus is ever likely to switch from topic to language, e.g. whenever a student asks the meaning of a word or a teacher corrects pronunciation, or gives an explanation of a particular usage. It does, however, represent an 'average' cline, from 'elementary' stages on the left to 'advanced' stages on the right.

We have completed our look at the more general section of this chart and will now go on to the lower section which is more specifically concerned with video.

We must remember at this point that I have limited this paper to the discussion of video playback facilities, excluding discussion on the uses of video for recording purposes. However, it would be impossible to give a clear account of the varying roles of video at the different stages without first clarifying *what* we shall be playing back; i.e. the software. So, I shall begin by summarizing briefly some types of video recordings that can be used to fulfil these objectives and roles, and used for the activities suggested at the bottom of this chart.

Purpose-made recordings for ELT. These can be home-made sequences recorded to illustrate particular language in use, (perhaps a sequence where instructions are being given, or a 'mini-lecture', 4 to 12 minutes long, to teach comprehension strategies), or bought from commercial sources, like the BBC.

'Authentic' material, i.e. programmes not made specifically for language teaching purposes, e.g. BBC Open University programmes and other educational programmes; features or documentaries, drama, comic or otherwise, cassettes of which are available on loan or on hire through

video libraries[6]; also in-house recordings, in existence in departments of your institution perhaps. Some, if not most, of these 'authentic' materials will, in fact, be scripted and/or much edited, so their degree of *linguistic* 'authenticity' is ever doubtful—a point to watch for.

Classroom-based recordings, e.g. of other classes of students playing language games, carrying out role-play or simulation activities, and other classroom-based activities that can replicate events (linguistic events) in the real world[7]. (These would mostly need to be in-house productions) (*Concept 7–9*), ELT films[8].

I am not however suggesting that only one particular type of software is suitable for one particular objective. Each type of programme may have several short sequences, each suitable for exploitation at a different stage for one or several different purposes. It is not the type of material, it is the length and size of unit used—as we have already discussed—that is important.

There is one proviso, however, which is that the subject matter, the message, is relevant and interesting for the students concerned; if a programme is thought to lack face validity, students will quite likely gain very little from watching even a short section of it. They will not feel like making a great effort to understand something in which they have little interest.

So now, having given some idea of the kind of video software we may have recourse to, I would like to continue by considering, in the light of those materials, the rest of the chart.

ROLES OF VIDEO

In this section of the chart I propose six tentative categories for roles for the use of video, which relate to the objective and units in the columns above. It has proved very difficult to choose suitably explicit titles for each role, hence the fairly lengthy exemplifications below each title. The categories suggested are not intended to be hard and fast: some roles will, at times in the lesson, inevitably overlap with one another; one role may become embedded within another. The distinctions, too, are not absolutely clear cut; there are grey areas in between. However, this does represent, as far as I know, the first attempt to define specific roles for video, and although there is room for improvement, I feel the resulting categories should be of practical use.

As you read the examples in each column, bear in mind the possible types of software that could be used for each. Consider, too, the possible adaptations you would have to make to suit your own students.

The categories proposed by Riley, p. 6, for the 'Role du Visuel' (see Figure 2 in *Implications for the Exploitation of Video in the ELT Classroom*) are not the same type of category as 'Roles of Video' here. Riley distinguishes six different functions of the visual component of video, and most of his six functions can be exploited, in different ways and for different purposes, at all the stages mentioned in this chart; we should not confuse the 'roles of the visual element' (i.e. in communication in general) with the 'roles of video' (i.e. for language teaching).

SEQUENCE LENGTH

The lengths of video sequence suggested here are approximate, but relate very closely to the UNITS of TEXT suggested above. For example, at an early stage, a sequence consisting of a single exchange, or short chain of exchanges is hardly likely to be longer than 30 seconds. At an intermediate stage, when one might ask students to read a passage of 3/4 page in length, or to do a listening comprehension of a text lasting 2 to 5 minutes, there is no pedagogic reason to ask them to study more than 2 to 5 minutes worth of text on video. (Of course, a video recording may be broken up by silences where the visual channel takes over for short spells so the actual playback time may be longer.) Further discussion of this point comes later, in section 4.

ACTIVITIES

This final section of the chart contains some examples of the one hundred and one ways to use video. Again, the activities outlined in each column can fulfil part of the objectives stated at the top of the same column, and so, at this point, one should refer vertically up each column so as not to lose sight of the other aspects. A key is provided alongside these activities: suggestions are made concerning size of group and initial patterns of interaction among students and vis-à-vis the teacher; these include pairwork, group work and teacher with class. Many of these activities could be adapted for self-access students. Suggestions are also made as to how the first showing(s) of the video can be done, with or without sound or picture. (This can help students to focus and concentrate on one channel at a time.) Implied in the brief outlines of the activities are the support materials that will be needed in addition to the video cassette, e.g. student hand-outs containing an introductory written text, or a set of jumbled pictures/main points to identify or rearrange, a matrix or flow chart to fill in, or perhaps even an audio tape to be compared with the information given by the video tape. Obviously the style of support materials you create will depend on the video programme itself as well as your teaching objectives; some video sequences, for example, lend themselves to matrix or flow-diagram representation, others do not. Ideas and techniques used for reading/listening comprehension and problem-solving and simulation activities will obviously be useful here. The important thing is that the activity should provide the opportunity for purposeful viewing; it should create a need for students to be actively involved in processing the information they receive. That is to say, an activity should demand an outcome which represents a useful achievement on the part of the students, such as the completion of a matrix that can subsequently be used as a basis for a written report, or the drawing up of a set of written instructions that could actually be used in real life or as one of the 'props' for a simulation activity involving, in this case, a trainee and an instructor. Activities like this, then, involve not only extracting information, but putting it to good use.[8] Only in trivial examination situations are people expected to answer comprehension questions, i.e. to extract information, for no other purpose than to show their level of understanding.

A practical exercise

Having now been acquainted with the contents of the chart, you might find it useful, in order to gain a working knowledge of it, to select some of the activities for video that are mentioned in this volume or those which you use yourself or have seen others use, and then try to map them on to the chart in the appropriate column, thus adding to the suggestions already there.

It should in fact be possible, given the information in this chart, and the examples of activities here, to generate many more such activities suitable for your own students, whose needs you are familiar with, bearing in mind the type of video software available to you that you can borrow, hire, buy or produce simply yourself.

2. Some Examples

Perhaps all these explanations in 1. above have seemed rather abstract, but these are, in fact, the procedures that most people follow when handling, for example, written texts. Let us take some examples and work them through.

It is useful to begin at the top of the chart by identifying what the language teaching objectives are for a specific group of students; let us take students with stage 4 objectives for these examples. These objectives we can understand more easily with reference to the language skills and types of material we are familiar with, for example, written texts; we can then apply the same principles to the exploitation of video materials, adapting where necessary. So, just as a good teacher who wanted to practise relevant micro-skills to help students recognize the structure of a text would first arouse students' interest in the theme of the chosen reading or listening extract by asking them to speculate and make predictions about the subject matter and its organization and/or presentation, based on the evidence given by title, review, or illustrations, etc. (thus creating a situation where students will want to read the passage to see if their predictions are fulfilled), the teacher with a video extract can do the same, either by showing students a copy of the relevant section from the film catalogue, or a brief review of the video extract such as one might find in a film review, or by showing the first 30 seconds of the video revealing the title captions, and then switching off. In order to get students from stage 2 onwards to read or listen purposefully, a teacher can previously set specific questions to which the students find the answers in the text, so that they process the information they receive in a systematic and evaluative way; the same can of course be done before showing a video extract. Just as we have techniques for teaching reading and listening comprehension strategies, we can apply the same basic principles to the teaching of strategies for 'viewing comprehension'[7], exploiting the text for its linguistic potential and relevant language teaching items. We must, however, remember that a 'video text' is a synthesis of the verbal and non-verbal, i.e. of sound and vision; the interrelations between these can vary from programme to programme and sequence to sequence. The visual channel can also be exploited linguistically, and often in conjunction with the aural channel.

With lower level students, practising the familiar set dialogues and simple role play situations, we could use video to fulfil objectives 1 and 2, e.g. using video as a model for a very short functional sequence (perhaps based on a single exchange), like making and accepting an offer, or as a target, illustrating a situation for a role play activity, like offering food and drink at a party, which would involve a series of exchanges, part of a 'transaction'.[9] When introducing a dialogue or role play in class without video, one needs to establish the context, the situation, the social setting, the status and roles of the characters and the register. This still needs to be done when using video, the only difference being that with video this can be more speedily and interestingly achieved owing to the presence of the visual channel. One could, for example, do this by using preliminary showings of the video sequence with volume OFF, followed by guided pair discussion.

In the same way as a good course designer and teacher would aim to integrate the main language skills as far as possible, (for example, promoting oral discussion before reading, leading on to further discussion then writing), one should not only integrate the video component, where it best fits, into the course as a whole, but also practise the 'viewing' skill in conjunction with the other language skills.

The principles behind techniques like Jigsaw listening and reading[10], or games like *Spot the Difference*[10] can equally well be applied to using video extracts; in order to help students to integrate skills by transcoding information and to read or view critically, one video extract could be used in conjunction with a similar but not identical written account of the same situation: half the group watches the video, while the other half (outside, or in another room) reads the written account; ensuing discussion between members of the two groups aims to establish the differences or piece together the whole story; these can then be recorded in writing, or in spoken form on tape, depending on the needs of the students. Thus students have read or viewed with the purpose of discussing and reporting orally what they have understood, the final purpose being to reach a consensus of opinion about the facts. In doing so, they have been fulfilling the objectives stated at 4 in the chart.

3. Summary of Ways to Use the Chart

We have seen, then, in section 2 how to adapt already familiar classroom techniques for use with video, having first identified what language teaching objectives we aim to fulfil by so doing.

I would like now to summarize the different ways in which this chart can be used.

3.1 Practical Video Use

We can either work up the chart, from the bottom, to check whether the activities we think of and like using in class do, in fact, fulfil stated objectives. Or, and this obviously is the ideal way, we can generate new activities of our own by working downwards through the chart, taking into account the language objectives (adapted where necessary to suit our own students), the units of text we have available on video, the possible roles of video, and sequence length; this procedure is likely to produce practical and innovative video use.

Many of us, however, will need to start in the middle of the chart. Due to the *ad hoc* fashion in which video has come into our lives and teaching institutions, we are often forced to start from what video materials we have available; and usually this also means what favourite programmes we have and know well and/or have transcriptions of (it is almost impossible to create good support materials without reference both to the script and to the screen). So in this case, it is a matter of relating what materials we already have (as well as what activities we already do) to the chart, to evaluate more objectively what we are doing, and seek new inspiration. In which case, we should start from UNIT and SEQUENCE LENGTH, identifying which sequences from our favourite video programmes best fulfil our OBJECTIVES—remembering what we have said about UNITS of discourse—then thinking about the possible ROLES of video at this stage, and finally selecting appropriate ACTIVITIES to exploit the language of the video sequence.

If we do not do this, there is the very grave danger of letting the machine master the man—and of our losing sight of our language learning objectives as the video ceases to be a language teaching tool and reverts to 'television', mesmerizing all present, encouraging active minds to slip into the passive, uncritical state that Mander[1] reports so vividly, that catatonic state that is the least conducive, apart from actually sleeping, to learning.

If you still do not believe that a 20–30 minute programme is too long for a language lesson, then sit down and transcribe it in full. As you do so, note down the 'teachable' language points. Then compare the length of text you have transcribed, and your list of possible teaching aims, with your usual reading/listening comprehension passage. (OK, it *is* easier to understand with the visuals, but is that the point?) Few language teachers would feel justified in letting students spend 20–30 minutes reading whole chapters of a book in class, or listening non-stop to a radio discussion for that length of time. Students could equally well do that outside valuable class time, just as they could all watch the same TV programme in the evening, for homework. Exposure to language *is* valuable, but class time can surely be better spent in examining in greater depth shorter sections of video/audio/written text, the size of the UNITS suggested in the chart, and exploiting them for specific linguistic purposes that will help students acquire strategies for comprehension and simple effective language for communication.

Students would probably question the purpose of a teacher regularly giving them 20–30 minutes of continuous silent reading in class. They do not yet question the purpose of silently watching 20–30 minutes of video because they can enjoy watching video for its own sake as they do at home.

3.2 Marketing Video

We have, in fact, now come round to the second problem, mentioned at the beginning of this paper, that of marketing video.

We have not thought hard enough yet about how to market video to our students as a teaching tool. The only way we can do this successfully is by making the students themselves thoroughly conversant with their learning needs and our language teaching objectives and the roles that video can fulfil in the classroom to help achieve those objectives. (This is an added reason for us, as teachers, to be perfectly clear in our own minds what these roles and objectives are.) Students' attitudes to the television screen in the classroom must be changed if video is to become a useful aid. Compare a video sequence to a reading text. It is strange to think that most students will quite happily read in class a decontextualized passage, an extract from some unknown work, and answer multiple-choice questions on it. They have grown so used to doing this they rarely demand to read the rest of the book (as they usually demand to see the rest of the programme), they do not complain at having to answer, aimlessly, a number of questions. Thus we have proof that students will accept the principle of short extracts for language study. Now, attitudes towards video are unlikely to change overnight, but if we, time and again, choose an interesting video sequence of a suitable length and complexity, contextualize it well, state our teaching objectives in such a way that our students understand, then get them to take part in two or three purposeful activities that have real outcomes and give our students a sense of personal achievement, how can we fail?

Notes and References

1. Mander, G. (1978) *Four reasons for the elimination of television*, unpublished paper.

2. This term was first used in this sense by Wachendorf, D. *Discourse Analysis in Foreign Language Teaching*, University of Birmingham M.Litt. thesis, where he explores the implications of focus shift more fully.
3. Definitions of these levels as stated by the RSA Board in relation to their Cert. TEFL; i.e. 'elementary'—students using a 'standard' first year course book; 'intermediate'—up to RSA Stage II or Cambridge FCE; 'advanced'—up to RSA Stage III or Cambridge Proficiency.
4. Basically this model is a hierarchical model with five ranks, each unit consisting of one or more units from the rank below; thus we have (descending order):

   INTERACTION
   TRANSACTION
   EXCHANGE
   MOVE
   ACT

   A detailed description of the original model can be found in Sinclair, J. McH and Coulthard, R. M. (1975) *Towards an Analysis of Discourse.* O.U.P. London: an updated summary in Coulthard, R. M. and Montgomery, M. (eds.) 1981, *Studies in Discourse Analysis*, London R.K.P.; applications to language teaching in Willis, J. D. *Applications of Discourse Analysis to Language Teaching*, University of Birmingham PhD. thesis.
5. On the advice of Hoey, M. For more on the structure of written discourse see Hoey, M. *On the Surface of Discourse*, University of Birmingham, unpublished.
6. One such catalogue of video cassettes is *The Video Source Book—U.K.* 1981, The National Video Clearing House, Inc., New York, USA, available from Bookwise Services Ltd., Catteshall Lane, Godalming, Surrey GU7 1NG.
   The Central Film Library, ILEA Learning Materials Services, (Bromyard Avenue, London W3 7JB) also operate a very reasonable video cassette hire service, and Dundee College of Education produce a catalogue of learning materials which includes video cassettes for purchase at very reasonable prices. Larger companies who produce training or promotion films are sometimes willing to loan them out on video cassette.
7. Riley, P. (1979) C.R.A.P.E.L., 'Viewing Comprehension—L'oeil écoute'. Also appeared in ELT Documents 1981. Special Issue *The Teaching of Listening Comprehension.*
8. I am grateful to J. McH Sinclair (University of Birmingham) for some stimulating discussion on this subject. What I have suggested here and elsewhere, though vital, still represents only a very incomplete view. See the materials produced for the University of Malaysia Spoken English Project. Also *Concept 7-9, Part Three, 'Communication': film and materials*, E. J. Arnold 1972.
9. *Functional Sequences* of this kind on video are currently being piloted experimentally by the British Council, Design, Production and Printing Department, London, with a view to publication.
10. Materials for language teaching produced initially by British Council ELTI. See *Listening Links*, Heinemann Educational, 1979, and British Council ELT film *Activity Days*, 1976.

TYPES OF VIDEO SOFTWARE: A USER'S EXPERIENCE

JOHN McGOVERN

Introduction

As the title implies, this will not be a theoretical article. Other articles in this volume have looked at video very much from the applied linguist's and educational technologist's point of view. Rightly, the authors have stressed the need to treat video in the same manner as other audio-visual aids and they have gone on to examine its properties and assess its strengths and weaknesses.

What I wish to do is to complement these articles by providing instances from my own teaching and materials designing experience, which I hope will clearly illustrate and reinforce many of the points made by these authors and, in addition, give an insight into how students react to certain types of video usage. My experience of video has been very much at the chalk-face. Having convinced myself early on of the value of video as a teaching aid, I have tried to explore the different ways it can be used and the viability of the different sources of software.

In some ways, then, this article will be no more than a succession of anecdotes. However, each anecdote will touch upon important topics concerning video usage e.g. hardware familiarization, software selection, methodology and it is hoped that the reader will be able to abstract from the anecdotes mistakes made and lessons learnt, which are of more general application.

1. First Encounters

I think the first time I saw a video-cassette recorder (VCR) was in 1975. The far-sighted headmaster at the London school where I was working had been quick to see the potential value to a school of this new technology. Unfortunately, he did not arrange for his teachers to be formally introduced to the machine. Like teachers the world over, the staff were very wary of yet another piece of apparatus being put between themselves and their students. As a result it stayed locked away in a cupboard, except for the odd occasion when an extra television set was needed. Then it was uncovered and led from its secret abode by the school technician, who was the only person confident enough to plug it in.

2. BBC ELT Series

I was somewhat disconcerted, therefore, on my arrival in 1976 at the British Council's teaching centre in Tehran to find most classrooms were equipped with VCRs. Video was being employed to supplement the language courses at the Centre, using programmes from the BBC English by Television series *On We Go* and *People You Meet*. Teacher resistance to the machines was soon overcome. A short familiarization course demonstrated that operating the VCR was not difficult. Perhaps the most crucial factor in teacher conversion to video, though, was the student reaction to video usage. No matter how banal the characterization, how feeble the story or how false the dialogue, the students patently enjoyed their 'turn for the video'.

However, after a time, teachers realized there were problems in using this kind of material. Firstly, students were quite content to sit and watch one programme after another. It was far too easy, with programmes lasting up to 20 minutes, for the lesson to turn into a period for *watching television* rather than a time for language learning. Secondly, these programmes had been designed for broadcast use and for use, if necessary, without a teacher. The television became the teacher. Not all of the teachers were happy with a change in their role which meant that they were no longer in control of the content or pace of their lessons but locked into a syllabus and methodology drawn up, perhaps, years previously, by a team in London for use worldwide. The design took no account of the particular group of students with whom the teacher was currently working.

This seemed to be a bad case of the tail wagging the dog. However, the hardware was too expensive to simply abandon and the teachers had begun to see that presenting the new language to the students on video had distinct advantages over presenting it through disembodied voices on audio tape or dialogues printed in textbooks. The students certainly seemed to find language learning via video a more interesting and enjoyable experience.

One could understand the student's viewpoint. Few of our language-using activities are conducted using just the audio channel. We obtain so many clues to meaning from the visual channel. By providing the student with both audio and visual signals we were making his language learning experience much closer in nature to his language using experience. For the first time in the language classroom he was being given the kind of support to comprehension he was used to in the real world.

It was decided, therefore, to persevere with video usage but to seek alternative sources of software.

3. Adapted Non-ELT Materials

Adapting materials designed for non-ELT purposes seemed an easy and obvious way out of the problem. So much filmed and video-recorded material, on a wide variety of topics and of a high technical quality is produced every year that it was thought that it must be possible to identify appropriate material and then, with some adaptation, slot it into the centre's courses. It was realized that, of course, this type of material, having been produced for native-speakers, would be too difficult for beginners and lower intermediate to follow. However, it was even possible with this new technology to record a completely new soundtrack to accompany the visual images. Heady days!

The centre had some success with adapted materials, the most notable of which was the adaptation of the *BBC Engineering Craft Studies* series. In 1977 the centre was asked to teach 330 technicians who were to go for technical training in Britain. A course was designed for them which included a large element of technical English.[1] As it was an intensive programme and therefore demanded as much variety of classroom activity as possible, a technical film was sought. This series seemed most appropriate. Not only was the content right but the series itself is 'particularly well-suited to language teaching since there is very often an obvious and direct relationship between the visual images and the spoken commentary.'[2]

The centre acquired the series on video tape for ease of operation in the classroom. The films were treated in units of approximately four minutes in order to ensure that the students were neither inundated with new language items nor given sufficient time to lapse into just picture-watching. Before showing the sequence, the teacher introduced some of the key tenses used in the commentary. The sequence was then shown in its entirety. After viewing, the students went to work on a host of support material which was designed to teach them how to express the technical concepts and linguistic notions and functions introduced in the sequence. Audio tapes of the spoken commentary were produced and later given to the students as it was felt that for listening for specific information audio tape was preferable to a video tape as it did not have a visual image to distract student attention. After completion of this practice stage, the sequence was shown again to review the pedagogic points made.

The video had three roles, therefore. First of all, it beautifully contextualized the new teaching items. Secondly, it 'offered a ready context for review of material that had already been practised under careful control.'[3] Thirdly, it enhanced student motivation by varying the classroom activity. 'The use of video or film can play a very important role, in that this, more effectively than any other medium, pushes back the walls of the classroom and shifts the forces of the lesson to the world outside'.[4]

Unfortunately it was not possible to adapt useful material like this for all or even most of the centre's courses. The sheer volume of filmed or video-recorded material that is produced every year can in fact become a disadvantage as it makes it difficult to know even where to begin to look for potential language teaching material. Secondly, overseas, it is not easy to gain access to material for viewing. More important than either of these two points, however, is that, for a variety of reasons, access is often restricted to certain types of material e.g. documentaries. Such types, as we have seen, have their uses but material showing *interaction* between speakers is perhaps more useful and certainly more relevant to those centres where the majority of students want primarily to improve their oral fluency. The number of 'theoretical productions' i.e. productions employing actors and therefore containing dialogue, which can be recorded or bought, is very limited.

So, though it was seen that adapted material had a useful role to play, *provided* it was properly exploited, it was also seen that it could not be the total answer to the problems posed by the software vacuum.

4. In-house produced material

Another possible option was then for the centre to produce its own video material. This option had obvious advantages. One could tailor the video material exactly to the centre's courses.

The Council was fortunate to be, by any normal language teaching institute standard, extremely well-equipped and staffed for video production. There were two portable video cameras, light and sound equipment, an editing suite, a graphics artist and a technician all at the disposal of an Educational Technology Officer with experience and expertise in video production. Several production projects were mounted but I only wish to discuss two—one an input into a general English course, the other into an ESP course. I will deal with the General English project first.

At that time the Tehran centre was developing for use in 4 teaching centres in Iran a beginner's course entitled Basic Oral Communication Skills (BOCS). The course was divided into 12 × 5 hour units and each unit focussed on a particular function e.g. greetings and introductions, and its related discourse network.[5]

For each unit a sequence or series of sequences showing the function being performed was recorded. The sequences were very short (approximately 1 minute) so as not to place undue strain on the student's memory capacity. They were used several times within a unit's work but each time for a different pedagogic purpose. First they were used for *elicitation*. With the sound turned off the students viewed the sequence. Having established the setting and the type of participants, the teacher elicited from them the language they thought was being used. With the sound turned up the sequence was then used for *presentation* of the language and presentation of the target performance the students were expected to attain by the end of the unit. Finally after the practice stage of the unit had been completed using audio and print materials, the sequence was brought back to aid the student in his preparation of the role-play and particularly to check on his appreciation of the non-verbal features of the interaction.

The video material was very successful. Video was being made to work for the teacher rather than the other way round. Its role was not to entertain or to teach but principally to present the learner with the new language much more richly contextualized than was possible using other aids. The setting, role and status of the participants was immediately obvious. The *total* behaviour of the participants was on the screen for use as a model. There was no hard evidence to prove video was a more effective presentation tool but it was obvious that it involved and hence motivated the students more than other available teaching aids.

There were, however, serious *problems*. The materials were very difficult to 'export' even to other Council centres in Iran. There were two reasons for this. First of all, the standard of acting was considered by teachers outside of Tehran to be so bad that they did not wish to use the materials. The actors in the sequences were ordinary teachers, not professional actors nor even practised amateurs. In the Tehran centre this did not seem to matter so much as the students knew the personalities involved. Secondly, the technical quality was also considered to be poor. By institutional standards, the video facilities in Tehran were excellent. However, it was not possible to obtain with good semi-professional equipment the broadcast standards television viewers have come to expect.

An even more serious problem was the amount of time it took to record, edit and reproduce the sequences. If it is accepted that an 8:1 time ratio exists between the preparation and actual classroom use of audio materials, the ratio must be 40:1 for video materials. Very few institutions can afford that amount of time for materials preparation. So though the BOCS video project had demonstrated the value of video it also proved, at least to me, that in-house production was also not the answer to the problem of how to fill the software gap.

I must be careful, however, not to suggest that in-house recording is always and everywhere an expensive waste of time as this is certainly untrue. In 1978 the Centre was asked to provide an ESP course for a group of students who were to be subsequently trained as educational technologists. Lectures were to play an important part in their training and so a lecture comprehension component was built into the language course. It was decided that lecture comprehension skills could best be taught using a simulation methodology and video seemed to be the most appropriate aid to employ. A series of recordings were made of mini-lectures on educational technology topics by the course designer. Each week the length of the lecture was increased until a 30-minute recording was made of a lecture given by the person who was soon to become the principal lecturer on their educational technology training course. In order to ensure the video material was properly used and exploited once again a lot of print and audio material was produced for use at the *pre-viewing, viewing* and *post-viewing* stages. This material focused on the lexis, content and especially the verbal and non-verbal discourse features of each lecture. A lecture is a much easier event to record than an interaction between several people and the technical quality was therefore of a higher standard than the BOCS material but it was still by no means broadcast standard. This did not seem to matter, however. The material was only designed for use within the institution and the advantages of the video material seemed to far outweigh the disadvantages. Video enabled the course designer to bring into the classroom material and tasks of immediate and obvious relevance to the students and allowed him to develop skills and strategies which would have been very difficult to teach as effectively using any other medium.

The point that I wish to make, therefore, about in-house recordings is not that they are an expensive waste of time but that everyone involved should be aware from the beginning of what kind of standard it is possible to achieve given the institution's facilities and resources. If that standard is acceptable then it is worthwhile considering production. Again one must not forget the time factor. Even a simple recording of a lecture using two cameras was surprisingly time-consuming and could only be justified by the belief that the material would be used for a succession of groups. Recording teaching material is not like making home movies. Students and teachers have higher expectations than members of a family or friends. It is necessary to plan the shots in order to ensure that the camera is picking up at each stage points which the teacher can later exploit. If one just points the camera at the action the product which results will in all likelihood be not only very boring and difficult to watch but also virtually unusable as teaching material.

5. Recording Student Performance

An obvious source of software but one which up to this point had not been tapped was to make recordings of students performing in the target language. I was reluctant to use video for this purpose for several reasons but principally because I was concerned about how the shy students, which one finds in any teaching group, might react to the public exposure such recording involved. However, after commencing work at the Council's English Language Teaching Institute in London in 1979 I was given reason to doubt whether my reluctance was justified.

Every year the Institute ran a *pre-sessional course* for overseas students. As part of the course test battery the students were interviewed at the beginning and end of the course. The interviews were recorded on video and then parts of both interviews were edited together and shown to the students on the final day of the course in order that they could assess their progress. The student reaction was interesting. They were genuinely keen to see the difference in their performance and thought that video provided them with as fair a record as was possible. It captured not only the improvement made in verbal fluency but also the improvement made in their ability to communicate. The students appreciated the two are not necessarily identical. It was decided, therefore, in the following year to extend this use of video to other course components.

Perhaps the best example to cite is that of the use of video in teaching *seminar skills*. A group of students, up to a maximum of eight, were given a topic to prepare. The topic chosen was usually both topical and moral e.g. euthanasia. One of the students was asked to give a short paper (3 minutes) to introduce the issue and the subsequent discussion (12–15 minutes) was recorded. The recording was then played back immediately and the students were asked to evaluate their contributions according to criteria previously agreed e.g. the relevance of their contribution, their ability to interrupt correctly and hold the floor.

The first time with each group was usually unsuccessful. Many of the students were unfamiliar with seminars as an academic event and virtually all of them were unused to the presence of a camera. By the end of the course, however, there was a distinct improvement in their performances which the students were most gratified to see. Their written feedback at the end of the course indicated that what they found useful was being able to *see* themselves operating in a foreign language. Of course, everyone gets a kick from seeing themselves on television and it was noticeable that some students 'dressed' for the occasion but I think there was more to it than that.

I remember the first time I saw myself teaching on video. It was a rude shock but a very worthwhile experience as I was made immediately and painfully aware of how I failed for a variety of reasons to 'make my point'. I knew what I was supposed to do but I was not aware of the fact that I was not doing it. The students were their own best critics. They realized very quickly that there was more to seminar participation than making grammatically correct statements and worked hard at making eye-contact, being brief and to the point and preventing others interrupting whilst they were still rightly entitled to the floor. There was no doubt too that the constant feedback that these recordings provided to them of their performance in the target language was a great boost to their confidence and hopefully enabled them to make a successful transition from operating in the safe environment of the language classroom to operating in the real world of the university. I feel sure that recording student performance has as important a role to play in language training programmes in the future as it has already acquired in, for example, management training programmes.

Again, however, there are constraints which have to be taken into account. Setting up the room, the lights, the camera and the sound equipment, even after one has become reasonably experienced, takes far more preparation time than most other classroom activities. Getting good sound quality is not easy when several people may be trying to speak at once and will probably mean the institute having to invest in more expensive sound equipment than it is used to.

6. Professionally Produced Software Designed for Institutional Use

The answer to the problems caused by using inappropriate but commercially available material had been to try and develop in-house recordings. That in turn, however, created other problems the most important of which were the technical quality of the finished product and the enormous amount of staff time video production entailed.

The next logical step, therefore, was to develop, initially for Council teaching centres, video material using professional actors and a professional production team. The development and production costs of such material arc high and so, in order to ensure that the software finally produced would be marketable, a research and piloting stage was built into the project.

During 1980, 20 sequences were produced and trialled in various Council centres. The sequences were designed to try and find answers to all sorts of questions both professional and technical. Did Centres favour using video to assist in teaching functional or structural items? Did they prefer skills-based material? What kind of material was suitable for different levels? Should one script everything, semi-script or simply let the actors improvise? What was the optimum length of a sequence? Which methodological techniques worked with the different types of sequence? Should one record on video tape or shoot on film and transfer to video?

Feedback from the Centres provided the answers to many of these questions and it was decided to go ahead in 1981 with the production of two cassettes, one for use primarily but not solely with beginners/false beginners and the other with intermediate to advanced students. An important feature that both projects had in common was that neither set of materials was meant to be a course or even the basis for a course. The purpose was to enable centres to supplement their programmes with a video element but not to supplant them.

The project aimed at producing software for use with beginners/false beginners was entitled *'Functional Sequences'*. A survey was made to identify the most common functions taught in the textbooks in use with students at this level in Council centres. Discourse networks were then worked out for ten of these functions. The networks covered the most likely moves and registers the student would have to handle at his level outside the classroom e.g.

Asking Permission

Permission Granted — Permission Refused

A 30 second–1 minute sequence was then scripted for each element of the network. The criteria for the choice of realizations for these functions were frequency of use and learnability.

So much for the linguistic rationale. The design also incorporated other features aimed at ensuring the sequences had as much *visual impact* as possible and also had *face validity* for the student. We wanted the student to believe that this was the sort of context in which he may have to operate and this was the type of person he may have to interact with.

Particular care was taken, therefore, in the choice of *settings*. The artificiality of the studio was dispensed with in favour of locations like shops, restaurants, railway stations, offices etc. Care was also taken in the choice of character shown using the language. There were many different types; young and old, rich and not-so-rich, strangers and friends, white and black. Though the sequences were totally scripted there was no attempt made to make actors indulge in foreigner-talk. Indeed, regional accents were deliberately included. It is hoped, as a result of the design that this material will not only provide motivating well-contextualized items in different registers to be presented by the teacher but also material useful in orientating students towards British society and culture.

No particular *methodology* was prescribed in the design of 'Functional Sequences'. However, an approach which works well is the one described earlier for the video input to the Basic Oral Communication Skills course in Tehran. The great advantage of this method is that it can be easily adapted in order to utilize these sequences with intermediate or even advanced students with whom it is very often necessary to quickly check that they can properly handle basic functions.

The second project was to produce materials for use with intermediate to advanced students and was entitled 'Viewing Comprehension'.[6] The aims and objectives for this project were very different from Functional Sequences.

The material consists of 10 unscripted sequences of between 3–8 minutes duration. Each sequence can best be described as a short story depicting an event. For example, one sequence shows an interview taking place for the post of librarian, another a man feeling ill and having to leave work and visit the doctor, another a man trying to change his hotel room. The aims of the material were threefold. Firstly, to provide a stimulus for discussion in order that students may develop their fluency skills. Secondly, to teach students to utilize all the signals provided by an interlocutor and not simply the verbal uses. Thirdly, to improve the student's ability to recognize and express certain attitudes.

The success of the materials is dependent upon the event being of sufficient interest to get the student to involve himself with the characters in the sequence, discuss their relative merits and predict the outcome of the interaction. What emerged very strongly from the trialling of the pilot material was that the most successful sequences were those in which the *characters* of the interlocutors made students react. In some ways this is not surprising. The success of many television programmes also hinges on exactly the same factor.

The people portrayed in ELT textbooks have names but no character. No attempt is made to give them one. They are only introduced in order to have the all-important words put in their mouths or to hold together a story-line which is also likely to be devoid of all interest. It is impossible for the student to have any feelings about them one way or the other. Given how long it takes one to build up a character and context in print it is not surprising, however, that ELT textbooks do not even attempt to do so but instead resort to ingenious though highly contrived ploys to make him speak. This is a great waste. We spend a large proportion of our waking lives thinking and talking about our attitudes to other people and the way they behave. Attitudes to other people are a very rich source for discussion and it is just as important in a foreign language as it is in a mother-tongue to be able to recognize, react and express one's reaction to, for example, someone being deliberately and unnecessarily rude. With video it is possible to depict both the character and the context in seconds.

This type of material which concentrates on eliciting the student's reaction to what he sees and hears on the monitor is breaking new ground in ELT and an effective methodology had, therefore, to be developed. The design for the 'Viewing Comprehension' sequences contains no prescribed method. In fact, as the sequences do not all follow the same pattern it would be impossible to do so. Perhaps though it would be best to illustrate one method which seems to work very well. I will take for the purposes of exemplification the job interview sequence.

The sequence opens with the first candidate for the post of librarian being interviewed by two interviewers. During the course of the interview one learns that she is married, middle-aged with lots of experience but few qualifications and is quite conservative in her approach towards library use. The second candidate is a complete contrast; young, single, virtually no experience but well-qualified and very 'with-it' professionally. The sequence ends with a short sequence showing the ensuing discussion between the two interviewers about the candidates. They fail to agree.

There are three distinct stages in the teaching of the sequence.

Pre-viewing – The students in groups are told that they are about to see an interview for the post of librarian and their task will be to decide which candidate to accept. In preparation they are asked to draw up their own criteria in order to guide their judgement.

Viewing – The students watch the first interview without soundtrack and, again in groups, record their first impressions. They then see it with sound and discuss the merits of the candidate. The same procedure is repeated for the second interview.

Post-viewing – The groups then make their choice and argue their case with other groups. Finally, the students see what the interviewers decided.

Conclusion

Functional Sequences and *Viewing Comprehension* have been used since their production with a considerable amount of success. I personally believe that the only real answer to the software problem are projects of this kind. However, though institutions have been quick to invest in the hardware, publishers seem to have been slow to believe that they are prepared to invest similar amounts in building up a software resource base. The climate of opinion does now seem to be changing and several publishers are beginning to test the video water. These are encouraging developments: the greater the choice available, the sooner video will claim its rightful place in the teaching of English.

Notes and References

1. For details of this course design and of the adapted materials produced see *Exploiting Authentic Audio-Visual Material in an English Course for Technicians* by J. D. Willis, an unpublished paper given at the 1977 Isfahan ESP Conference and available from the Central Information Unit, British Council.
2. *op. cit.*
3. *op. cit.*
4. *op. cit.*
5. An amended version of this course by J. D. Willis is forthcoming from Longmans.
6. A term coined by Riley. See 'Viewing Comprehension: L'oeil écoute' in ELT Documents *The Teaching of Listening Comprehension* 1981.

VIDEO APPLICATIONS IN ENGLISH LANGUAGE TEACHING

JACK LONERGAN

Introduction

The suitability of television as a medium for bringing a living language to learners is undoubted. The dynamic combination of sound and vision can bring an air of reality into the classroom. The wealth of visual information available can convey the atmosphere of another culture, can show para-linguistic aspects of communication; the techniques of television can present material to learners in ways quite beyond the resources of the language teacher.

Harnessing the power of the medium for language teaching and learning, however, can present educational institutions and teachers with many problems. Making and transmitting television language programmes, or showing them on video tape, are subject to restrictions and constraints which can be in conflict with language learning aims.

This article looks at some of these problems involved in the classroom use of broadcast materials, and offers some practical examples of the use of video in class with language courses.

1. Language Programmes as Television Programmes

Language programmes are usually broadcast as part of a series. The programmes may be watched by learners in their homes (for self-study or as part of an institutional course), or in class if the lesson coincides with the broadcast times. These obvious facts have implications for the teacher and learner.

Firstly, the broadcast is ephemeral. The input from a broadcast is short-lived and usually one-way. Viewing time should therefore be used well by the learners and exploited by the teachers; the programme makers should bear this in mind when planning the broadcasts and accompanying written materials, if any. This unfortunately is not always the case, as shown by the examples discussed below.

Secondly, a broadcast series has its own tempo – the programmes are usually broadcast at regular intervals, and sometimes with repeats. The tempo of the broadcasts may be different from the speed at which the language class wants to deal with the material. The programme makers need to build into the series opportunities for teachers and learners to revise or take stock, or even to move out away from the central material and develop independently a particular theme.

These characteristics of the broadcast programmes make various demands on the teacher. If the programmes are watched by the learners at home, and there is a taught course linked to the programmes, then the teacher has the problem of relating the home-viewing of the learners to the classroom teaching in the institution. A similar effort is required from the learner, in that the best use must be made of the home viewing time; but home viewing means no teacher and no chance for feedback from learner to instructor. Viewing, therefore, must be prepared, structured and followed up if the best use is to be made of the programmes.

Having the programmes available on video tape for replay during class time presents the teacher with different, though related, problems. The video offers the obvious advantages of stop/start facilities, rewind/replay, sound on/off, and a stop frame, with possibly a slow motion control. This in turn means that the nature of the viewing experience is also quite different from home viewing. It is not enough to treat the video recorder merely as a convenient machine which enables broadcast programmes to be seen independently of transmission times. Watching video requires careful preparation, structuring and follow up; above all, however, it implies selection. The home viewer of a television transmission must watch the non-stop showing of a programme—straight through, no pauses or repeats. The same programme on a video tape can be shown in small selected segments. These segments can be exploited in a wide variety of ways, leading to language practice and language learning under the guidance of the teacher.

The problem of selecting material and linking it to classroom work is especially great if the language programme on video is an extra component, added to the main course which the class is following. The teacher must know the video material well, and by suitable preparation provide the links into and out of the main course (although video material can be very well used to initiate group discussions or project work, for example, that deliberately take the learners outside the confines of the main course).

Some practical examples illustrating these points are given in the last section of this article.

2. The Educational Role of Language Programmes on Television

Having language programmes stored on video tape has many advantages for educational institutions and teachers. Yet the vast majority of language programmes are made for public broadcasting; the programme makers are producing television—which is broadcast, and seen by many—and not video tapes—which are not broadcast, and seen by few. Part of the justification for this is that television can and should play a major role in education. As one observer has put it: 'Broadcasting offers blanket coverage. It therefore helps to overcome regional and social barriers more quickly than other means. The educational programmes offer instruction for everyone—without the constraints of travelling or local living conditions, and in so doing further educational justice and educational opportunity'.[1]

It is worth looking at this justification more closely, to see how valid it is for educational programmes on television, and particularly for language programmes.

Television can usually offer blanket coverage, but this does not mean that the maximum number of potential learners is reached. The constraints of television schedules—and the generally low priority given by the broadcasting authorities to educational television—mean that many people can never watch at the times when programmes are broadcast. Frequent repeats may be necessary to achieve high viewing figures; very few educational courses on television are given frequent repeats. Most individual learners do not have domestic video recorders. Only educational institutes, or similar bodies such as learning circles, can provide the facilities for taping, storing and showing again the educational programmes.

Language programmes must be designed to reach a specific target audience. No matter how wide-ranging the target area is, the programmes will have to assume something about the learners' pre-knowledge of the language. General interest programmes for advanced discussion might attract a most diverse audience; but real beginners are definitely excluded if they are watching the programmes as television broadcasts. The same beginners might be able to use parts of the programmes—the vision only, or selected bits of dialogue, or certain short sections, for example—given time for preparation by a teacher, and facilities for recording and selecting from the programme—which will usually mean a video recorder.

Perhaps more pertinent than the level of a language programme is the degree of learning that is likely to take place, watching programmes on television. There is a restricted amount of subject matter suitable for television teaching only, with no other material being used for instruction. The Open University in Great Britain recognizes this: the television presentations of a decade ago have given way to integrated teaching units. The television programmes are reinforced with pre-viewing materials, with reference points during the programme, and with follow up activities—usually requiring personal contact with a course tutor. It is perhaps self-evident that no learner of a foreign language will acquire communicative fluency in that language by receiving television instruction only (more controversial is the success of self-study language courses, a topic outside the scope of this article).

A further consideration is the promotion of educational justice and opportunity. Clearly, the public broadcasting of an educational programme is an important part of this. It is equally clear that resources are needed to complement the television component of what must be essentially multi-media courses. The other course components may be just a teacher, who works with a small circle of learners. Or course components can be many and various, including radio programmes, course-books, audio-cassettes for classroom use and for home study, homework books—and a teacher. The provision of these resources may be a matter for the relevant authorities or interest groups, or be the responsibility of a group of learners. Whichever, finance, organization and time are needed; these are not yet available to every potential language learner.

It seems then that for language programmes on television to be most successful in achieving their aims, they must be considered in the context of complementary support facilities; for the vast majority of learners, this means any one of a range of educational institutions: schools, colleges, industrial training units, adult education classes, holiday courses, and the like. The educational institutions should complement the broadcast television programmes all the more effectively if there is liaison and cooperation between the institutions and the broadcasting authorities.

3. Liaison Between Broadcasting Authorities and Educational Institutions

Successful cooperation between the broadcasting authorities and educational institutions should in the long term bring benefits to the learners—that is, the viewers of the programmes. By being involved at all stages of the planning and production (and then transmission) of a language programme, institutions should be better able to provide teachers with the information and resources needed for successful teaching. If teachers have access to the information they require about television language programmes, then they should be in a position to positively help the language learning of their students.

It is regrettable that this cooperation is often not forthcoming. One difficulty lies in identifying what are the real needs of a disparate group of educational institutions. However, a greater difficulty can be the disregard by the broadcasting authorities for the expressed needs of various users of the programmes.

At a national conference held in the UK in May 1980 to discuss the use of the media in language teaching, educationalists from all over the country drew attention to key areas where close cooperation and liaison between educational institutes and the broadcasting authorities was desired.[2] These areas included:

—full transcripts of all dialogues and commentaries in language pro-

grammes, with stills from the programmes to illustrate the style or idiom of the programmes
- advance promotional cassettes of new television programmes, with excerpts from the programmes, and, if possible, an example of how the programmes might be linked to classroom teaching
- access to video taped copies of programmes before public transmission for both planning and teacher training
- consultation with educational bodies about transmission times
- provision of better teaching materials to accompany the programmes, with special emphasis on notes for the teacher.

Compared with the provision expected from the publishers of written materials and audio cassette materials, these demands seem modest enough. However a lack of finance, a low level of priority, and even a lack of sympathy for the educationalists' points of view, all mean that broadcasting authorities rarely meet these needs when producing language programmes.

This problem of a lack of liaison is not confined to the UK or to language programmes. A member of an adult education media institute in Germany has written: 'Despite regular and frequent contacts with the authorities, it is difficult to get any detailed advance information about new multi-media projects. At most, isolated instances of cooperation from interested production staff provide some information; chance and personal contacts seem to determine what multi-media packages are being produced—a deplorable situation, and one which even an organization such as the Gesprächskreis Medienverbund (Multi-media Discussion Group) can do little to change'.[3]

As far as EFL programmes overseas are concerned, it is not uncommon for broadcasting authorities to take, for example, a BBC English by Radio and Television series, and broadcast the programmes on television without any consultation with educational authorities in the country.[4]

One reason for this lack of liaison might be differing views about the role of the teacher vis-à-vis language programmes on television. Television as a medium is acknowledged to be very powerful; the television language programmes themselves are of course central to this discussion. However, the television language programmes cannot be seen as the mainstay of the language learning process, for reasons outlined above. The teacher retains the central role, whether as didact, guide, facilitator or animateur.

4. The Task for the Teacher Using Broadcast Materials

To emphasize the central role of the teacher in the learning process using broadcast materials is not an attempt to put teachers on a needless pedestal. In many ways, it serves rather to raise the lowly self-esteem of many teachers, when confronted by broadcast materials. There is often the view that the strength of television as a medium, the electronic techniques it can use, and its power to attract, amuse and motivate an audience can all overshadow the humble teacher. The television takes the glory, and the teacher is left with the humdrum practice material.

It is usually inexperience, perhaps with a sense of awe of the technology which leads teachers to these views. In fact the teacher's role is central because the teacher has to relate the broadcast materials to the language learner's needs.

If the language programme is broadcast for home viewing, then the teacher's task is to prepare the learner for the home viewing, to structure that viewing, and to provide exploitation and follow-up in the classroom. The learners must not come to the television programmes with the passive frame of mind too often associated with domestic television; it is largely the task of the teacher to promote active viewing. To do this successfully, the teacher needs transcripts at least, and video taped copies of the programmes if possible. Secondly, the teacher must relate the home viewing of the television programme to the classroom teaching. The shared experience of the learners should be used for everybody's advantage in the classroom. It can often happen that the teacher is unable to see a programme before meeting the learners for their lesson; this creates an unusual but welcome situation for the EFL classroom: the learners have a genuine shared experience in English which the teacher knows nothing about.

If the language programme is available on video, then the task of the teacher involves careful selection of sequences for showing in class, as well as devising suitable language practice activities as follow-up work on the sequences. When video material is used as an adjunct to another course, then suitable links must be forged between the main course and the video material.

Consideration for the learner is also important. Just as many teachers are in awe of complicated technology, so many learners may feel daunted by television and video presentations. These learners must appreciate the medium as what it is: admittedly powerful, but no more than an extra aid for language teaching and learning. When introducing video taped programmes to learners for the first time, any tasks associated with viewing should be deliberately simple. The learners must gain in confidence, and feel that they are in command of the medium. When a style of learning from television has been established, then more complicated tasks can be attempted. In time, some of the responsibility for the selection of material, and associated tasks, can be devolved to the learners. The most extreme example of this might be where learners use complete studio facilities to write and record for later viewing and exploitation their own project material: a playlet, a documentary, or a discussion, for example.

The examples in the next section are meant to show the practical application of the points mentioned above. Further, they illustrate some of the many ways in which a video recorder can be used in class. As the exemplification of principle is the main aim, the examples are generally simple in construction, and not every aspect of every example is highlighted. It is for the reader to infer what is relevant for a local situation, and transfer the principles to that situation. The examples are taken from two courses published by BBC English by Radio and Television, to show the use of video at different levels: beginners, and advanced English for business.

5. Practical Examples

Developing Viewing Guides

Viewing Guides have two main purposes: to focus the learners' attention on certain sections of the programmes; and to provide a link between home viewing and classroom activities. Viewing guides involve comprehension skills, but are not designed to test these skills; they should guide the viewer during the programme. The level of difficulty should be such that most learners in the class can successfully complete the task when viewing alone.

The following examples are taken from materials developed to accompany *Follow Me*.[5] They illustrate how at beginners' level, active viewing tasks must concentrate on only small sections of the programme. The three guides in Table 1 are for a fifteen minute television programme.

The same focusing techniques can be used at higher levels, for example with advanced students of business English. The following grid[6] (Table 2) can be used with Episode One of *The Bellcrest Story* (BBC English by Television) to focus attention on the presentation of the characters in the series.

The slightly different skills required of the learner in each viewing guide help to maintain interest through variety. If a video recorder is available in class, then the guides can also be used in class. If viewing takes place at home, then the guides are one way of linking the common experience of the learners with the lesson in the classroom. The viewing guides can be used to initiate a new phase in the lesson, drawing at the same time on the motivating influences of the television programme.

Exploiting the Situation

The video presents the learners with a total situation. The sound track carries the language used in a scene, as well as background noises which add to the situation. Vision allows the setting to be seen and understood, and for para-linguistic features of communication to be appreciated.

Learners can practise speaking in situations which are presented to them by

1. Studio: At the customs ref. B1: to precede 1.1 Dialogue

What's in the priest's suitcase?	☐ a bottle of gin	☐ soap	☐ oranges
	☐ a bottle of milk	☐ milk	☐ apples
	☐ a bottle of medicine	☐ whisky	☐ clothes
	☐ a bottle of wine	☐ make up	☐ keys
	☐ a bottle of perfume	☐ toothpaste	☐ cigarettes
	☐ a bottle of coca-cola	☐ marijuana	☐ sandwiches

2. Studio: In the country ref. B1: to precede 2.2 Dialogue

What colour are the rivers, roads and grass on the map?

	black	white	blue	red	yellow	brown	green
rivers							
roads							
grass							

3. Studio: London quiz ref. B1: to precede 3.3 Read and speak

This is the Tower of London. How old is it?	Is it	☐ 500 years old? ☐ 700 years old? ☐ 900 years old?
This is the River Thames. How long is it?	Is it	☐ 238 kilometres long? ☐ 338 kilometres long? ☐ 438 kilometres long?
This is Big Ben. How high is it?	Is it	☐ 78 metres high? ☐ 88 metres high? ☐ 98 metres high?

Table 1. *Viewing guides for TV unit 7,* **Follow Me**

the video. By stopping the film and/or turning the sound down, learners can be invited to say something which is valid for the situation shown on the video. What the learners say is not necessarily a repeat of a model from the video, as the following two examples in Tables 3 and 4 show.

The first example (Table 3) is from Unit 19 of *Follow Me.* At this low level, learners are given a chance to respond to the video and teacher's questions, and use indirect speech without the constraints of a formal drill.

At a more advanced level, learners need to appreciate—and practise—the difference between apparent meaning and implied meaning. In this example

Names	Bellcrest	Electrovans	The Bank	Other	Position
Maurice Downes	x				Mangaging Director and .....
Sir Frederick					
George Hanson					
Paul Malone					
Tom Driver					
Edward Needham					
Charles Spence					
Donald Williams					
Bob Orpenshaw					

Table 2. *From The Bellcrest Story (BBC)*

from *The Bellcrest Story*, Downes, the managing director, does not really agree with Malone's proposals. After the learners are familiar with the contents of the scene, the exercise in Table 4 can be used.

Intonation, stress and even gesture are very important in this scene. By using just the stop/start facility on the video recorder, the teacher can let the learners practise—by imitation—Downes's remarks, before going on to the exercise outlined in Table 4.

A variation is the type of exercise where the learner must watch and listen for specific uses of language: the setting, paralinguistic information and language used provide the clues. Table 5 gives a further exercise from Casler (*op. cit.*); based on *The Bellcrest Story*:

Introducing Role Play

Language learners need to be familiar with the setting, characters, speech intentions and language used before they can successfully role play. This familiarity can be quickly gained by a presentation of a scene on video. In programme 7 of *Follow Me* there is a scene at the British customs. The Customs Officer asks a traveller to identify the various things wrapped up in his luggage. The scene can be played several times, and then broken into convenient sections.

By using the pause button to stop the programme, the teacher can create a situation in which the learners reply to the Customs Officers questions. Exact repetition of the language in the film is neither required nor possible; within the framework of known language, the learners should give a response suitable to the scene.

Many learners, particularly adults, are often reluctant to role play. Watching the actors on a television screen 'can provide an escape route for learners

AD SPOT: Long John Silver, Ann Boleyn, Nelson

VCR PLAYS: scene shown once completely
STOP
REWIND

SOUND OFF
VCR PLAYS
PAUSE BUTTON

(Passer-by):	*(He needs a leg)*
Teacher:	*What does he need?* (pointing to Long John Silver)
Learners:	*A leg/He needs a leg.*

FRAME RELEASE

PAUSE BUTTON

(Passer-by):	*(She needs a head)*
Teacher:	*What does she need?* (pointing to Ann Boleyn)
Learners:	*A head/She needs a head.*

FRAME RELEASE

PAUSE BUTTON

(Passer-by):	*(He needs an arm – and an eye)*
Teacher:	*What does he need?*
Learners:	*An arm/An eye/He needs an arm/He needs an eye*

FRAME RELEASE

PAUSE BUTTON

(Long John Silver):	*(I don't need a leg)*
Teacher:	*What did he say?*
Learners:	*He said he doesn't need a leg.*

FRAME RELEASE

PAUSE BUTTON

(Ann Boleyn):	*(I don't need a head)*
Teacher:	*What did she say?*
Learners:	*She said she doesn't need a head.*

FRAME RELEASE

PAUSE BUTTON

(Long John):	*(I don't need an arm – nor an eye)*
Teacher:	*What did he say?*
Learners:	*He doesn't need an arm/He doesn't need an eye*

Table 3. *Follow Me, Unit 19, Media Teaching Manual*

TEACHER starts the video recorder
Malone: Well, there's no doubt about the obvious solution to our short-term problems—that is, to concentrate on product lines which bring in the quickest returns and the largest profits.

TEACHER turns sound down
(*Downes:* Is that what you suggest we do?)

TEACHER stops the video recorder; LEARNERS respond to the situation
Learner 1: You're not suggesting that, are you?
Learner 2: Is that what you think we should do?

TEACHER turns sound up and restarts video recorder
Malone: Not exactly. I recommend that we should look after our regular customers as well as possible. But we must pay special attention to those customers who are likely to bring in our long-term profits.

TEACHER turns sound down
(*Downes:* What's the feeling about Paul's proposal?)

TEACHER stops the video recorder; LEARNERS respond to the situation
Learner 4: What do you think of this proposal?
Learner 5: Well—I don't know—what do you all think?
Learner 6: I wonder what you think of Paul's proposal.

TEACHER turns sound up and restarts video recorder (and so on).

Table 4. *The Bellcrest Story, Episode 6*

Episode Nine: ***Exercise Four:*** A lot of attitudes, opinions, and feelings are expressed in the brief exchange between Downes and Malone. Watch the segment again and listen for examples of the following:

1 Expressing pleasure
2 Expressing displeasure
3 Expressing opinion
4 Expressing disagreement
5 Accepting an argument
6 Expressing certainty
7 Expressing doubt

This particular activity is only part of a larger exercise which requires the learner to identify people through attitudes and opinions expressed during a dialogue of the episode. Hence, the first part is the information activity and the second part, illustrated above, is the function activity.

Table 5. *The Bellcrest Story, Episode 9*

from their own inhibitions. It is easier and as valid to imitate or ham the actor on the screen than to attempt one's own version'.[7]

When the class is familiar with the scene, and has practised half the responses in the situation as presented by the video, then the role play proper can begin. Shy or weak students can be invited to act as travellers (in this example) who are waved through the Green channel without having to talk to the Customs Officer; this active, but non-speaking role can be an introduction to role playing, while more able students have speaking parts—all modelled on the scene in the video film.

Questions and Discussions

The visual element of language programmes on television or video can provide great interest for learners. Style of dress, manners, landscape, street scenes, buildings, food markets—the atmosphere of a foreign country can be conveyed by the film. Most visual sequences in any television film can be used for language learning, as the basis for discussion and questions. The following example (Tablc 6) shows how a scene from a programme can be used by the teacher to start a discussion about an aspect of English life. It is from *Follow Me*, Unit 23, and the sequence was filmed outside the studio on location: a 'Loc Spot'.

Asking questions is an activity which is hard to practise with learners in a classroom. The stimulus of a language programme on video, however, can offer ideal material for such practice. Further, by putting the responsibility for selecting an interesting film sequence onto the learners, the teacher can increase the commitment of the learners to the language activity, and so create a better environment for learning.

The teacher should play a sequence of film about, for example, a trip across London in a taxi. At any time, the learners can interrupt, ask for the film to be stopped by the teacher or another learner, and then ask questions about something interesting that has been seen. The ensuing dialogue can take place among the learners, with the teacher monitoring rather than leading the discussion.

Summary

Broadcast programmes, available on video, are obviously a tremendous additional teaching and learning aid. The examples given above have concentrated on either the home viewing situation, or aspects of video programmes that draw on both sound and vision. The video recorder can be used in a far wider variety of ways. It can complement many uses of realia, flashcards, overhead projector transparencies, wall charts, slide projectors, film loops and audio cassettes. Most of the proven techniques of using visual and audio aids in language teaching can be adapted for use with the video recorder in

A major aim of language courses such as FOLLOW ME is to enable learners to freely discuss their own opinions about topics of interest. The example chosen for this unit concerns housing. Few non-English speaking countries have an approach to housing similar to that in Britain. For example, very few people rent houses or flats: those who do tend to be very rich, or of an age or outlook which means that they will be looking for new accommodation within a year or two. Nearly half the population live in council houses (with subsidised rents) or in privately owned houses. The following Loc Spot shows typical young buyers on a new English private housing estate.

LOC SPOT: Looking for a new home

VCR PLAYS

PAUSE BUTTON: stop at very first view of housing estate

Discussion points:	Housing estate – what sort of people live here? Houses – semi-detached, probably five rooms with a garage, and a garden front and back. Open plan layout – no fences or hedges at the front, but probably at the back.

FRAME RELEASE

Husband:	*This is the place. Let's go and look at some houses.*
Wife:	*I don't know. I think we have to tell someone if we want to see the houses.*

PAUSE BUTTON

Discussion points:	Young couple – what do they work as? Who buys houses like this in Britain? (Probably young white-collar workers, teachers, company representatives).

FRAME RELEASE

Husband:	*All right. Let's got to the sales office.*

PAUSE BUTTON: showing 'sales office' sign

Discussion points:	Sales office – what services are offered by the builders or estate agents? (Probably arrangements for a mortgage – on new estates 90–95% of price – as well as help with legal aspects of buying a house).

Table 6. *Follow Me, Unit 23*

class; but rather than supplant other aids, the video recorder offers the chance to extend these techniques with a new medium.

However, if teachers the world over are going to be able to use broadcast language programmes to their best advantage, then the required cooperation between teachers, educational institutes and broadcasting authorities must be forthcoming. The present writer was fortunate to receive—after many misunderstandings and much discussion—the fullest cooperation from BBC English by Radio and Television, Longman Group Ltd and the German television authorities when preparing training materials for teachers of the multi-media course *Follow Me*. This level of cooperation should be maintained and regarded as standard. Teachers of English overseas should make their voices heard by broadcasting authorities using language programmes—and remember that 'in the end, it is you, as a teacher, who will work out through experience your own best way of using a course'.[8]

Notes and References

1. From a report on multi-media education programmes in Austria in *Newsletter, European Bureau of Adult Education*, The Netherlands, Autumn, 1981.
2. The conference held at Stoke Rochford, was organized jointly by the Centre for Information on Language Teaching and Research (CILT) and the Continuing Education department of the BBC. The conference discussed the use of the media in teaching modern languages in the UK, and EFL overseas. Full reports of the conference are in a special issue on the use of broadcast material in language teaching of the *British Journal of Language Teaching*, Vol XVII, Nos. 2 & 3, Winter 1980.
3. From a report on multi-media educational programmes in the Federal Republic of Germany in *Newsletter, European Bureau of Adult Education, op. cit.*
4. The German-speaking Swiss television service set up a series of information and training programmes for teachers in adult education using *Follow Me*, a BBC English course for beginners. Two years later, in 1981, the French-speaking service broadcast adapted programmes without any liaison with French-speaking adult education institutes. Consequently, in contrast with the good example available, no institutes were ready to run courses, and no teachers properly prepared to run them.
5. National teaching training programmes in Austria and West Germany, preparing teachers to work with a new multi-media beginners course in English, led to the development of a detailed handbook on teaching the *Follow Me* course: Gaderer, H. & Lonergan, J. (eds), *Media Teaching Manual*, Austrian/West German Associations of Adult Education Institutes, Vienna/Frankfurt, 1980. The many components of *Follow Me* are published by BBC English by Radio and Television, and Longman Group Ltd.
6. The grid is from Casler, K. (1980) Video Materials in Language Learning, *Modern English Teacher*, **8** (2).
7. LONERGAN, J. (1980) 'Using television to motivate adults to role-play in a foreign language', *Perspectives on Academic Gaming and Simulation 5*, Kogan Page, London.
8. *Using Video in the Classroom* (1981) BBC English by Radio and Television, London.

USES OF VIDEO RECORDING IN AN INSTITUTION

MARGARET ALLEN

Introduction

A video camera is not a new method of training teachers. A ridiculously obvious statement perhaps but we do need to beware of confusing the tool with the technique. With a new resource we need to go through a stage of exploring potential and exchanging ideas but there is always a danger that the new resource will become an end in itself rather than a means to achieving learning objectives. With this caveat, this article aims to pass on some ideas drawn from a range of institutions which are using video cameras.

In order to discuss the uses of video in an institution more precisely, I find it helpful to delineate four main areas, derived from this matrix:

Video System \ Type of Programme	Teacher Training	Direct Teaching
Playback	1	2
Own recording	3	4

Figure 1. *Uses of video in ELT programmes*

On the vertical axis a distinction is made between a video playback system (recorder or player linked to monitor or receiver) and a system which includes a video camera. I include within the playback system the ability to copy material onto a video recorder and by 'own recording' I mean the production of your own material.

The distinction made on the horizontal axis is an obvious one to make. Not all institutions run both types of programme; those that do might find that they think of their video camera as belonging exclusively to one 'box', when in fact it has applications in another.

Most of the papers in this volume have been concerned with the box two area. I am going to consider boxes three and four: I shall discuss possible uses of a video camera in a teaching programme and in a teacher training programme, in relation to the time, equipment and expertise needed to undertake different types of production. Figure 2 summarizes the uses I shall consider:

3 Teacher training	4 Direct teaching
1. to record teacher performance 2. to record events relevant to trainees 3. to produce specially designed ELT teacher training material	1. to record student performance 2. to record raw data 3. to produce specially designed ELT teaching material

Figure 2. *Boxes 3 and 4 of Figure 1 matrix*

A brief word about the technical side: if an institution wants to have a recording facility, the basic choice is between a portable single camera system and a small two camera studio with simple controls. An editing facility may also be necessary. I have discussed these choices elsewhere[1] and will not go into technical detail here. Nor do I intend to discuss the provision of technical services such as maintenance and repair, essential though these are, except to stress that there is a difference between the operation of equipment and its maintenance. The former skills are not difficult to acquire and the more teaching staff are familiar with video cameras, the more they are likely to use them. This paper is concerned with what they will use them for.

1. Uses in Teacher Training

1.1 Recording Teacher Performance

Institutions most commonly give 'teacher training' as their reason for acquiring a video camera and the video camera's function as an 'objective eye', which lets us see ourselves as our students see us, has obvious applications in a teacher training programme. However even this use of a video camera needs more careful consideration than it is sometimes given.

Video is very commonly used as a tool to provide feedback in a microteaching programme, but the introduction of video recording of teachers is not the same as the introduction of microteaching principles. In many microteaching programmes trainees teach five or ten minute lessons to very small groups of learners, with the focus on one particular skill. The trainee then uses a record of the lesson to measure his/her achievement in the practice of that skill. A video camera provides a convenient way of recording the trainee's performance. It is a useful tool, but it is nothing more than that and it is not the only way of recording performance, although it is perhaps the most effective one.

In some institutions a video camera is used to record normal classes. These recordings are then viewed by the teacher who was recorded, and in some cases may be discussed with a tutor or senior colleague. This can be a useful way of helping teachers analyse their own performance objectively but it is not microteaching and reasons for doing it need to be thought through. It is time-consuming to record a whole lesson and then view the whole recording. It can also be time-wasting if a trainee views his/her own lesson without any guidance as to criteria to be applied. It is not necessary to introduce a micro-teaching programme to justify the video recording of classes but it might help to adapt some of its practices: for example, it is good discipline to specify each time the aspects of a lesson which are to be focused on and it is also necessary to train the viewing teacher in ways of assessing specific points in the lesson, if viewing sessions are to be effectively used.

The mechanics of recording classes are relatively simple—a camera fixed to the wall or set up in a corner can be switched on and off by the teacher and will record enough of what goes on for the teacher to view and recall details of the lesson through the camera's objective eye. Used in this way, the camera makes it possible for an in-service training programme to become trainee-operated to a large extent. The tutor can help each teacher draw up an individual list of skills to be practised, along with a list of criteria by which improvement could be measured. Teachers then concentrate on one skill at a time, recording and assessing their own performance, with the option of asking the tutor to view when they feel the need for help and guidance. The video recording helps recall the reality of the classroom and allows tutor and trainee to use their time in the most effective way.

1.2 Recording Events

One use of television in education is to bring to the learner the views or knowledge of eminent people with whom they could not otherwise have any contact. Institutions can use their video recording facilities in this way. There are sometimes guest lectures or specialist seminars which cannot be repeated every year but which are of wide relevance and interest. Some institutions make it a practice to video record these sessions for the benefit of those who missed them and perhaps, too, for next year's trainees. Provided the speaker does not object to being recorded, this seems a useful idea, but it is very necessary to check that these recordings are in fact used. Experience suggests that the recordings of such events may be done routinely—it is obviously such a good idea—but no one then checks whether or not anyone does in fact view the recordings.

Teacher trainers sometimes play this kind of recording in later training sessions. There is however quite a difference between sitting through a one-hour lecture in the flesh and watching the same lecture, unadapted, for one hour on a small screen. It will most probably be necessary for the trainer to spend some time selecting suitable passages, and in this case the ability to edit out useful sequences adds a lot to the smoothness of presentation. Alternatively library viewing may be programmed in to a teacher training syllabus, and possibly a viewing guide prepared to help a trainee select relevant sections. If recordings are to be available for self access in this way, then teachers must know about them, machines must be available for viewing at times convenient to teachers, and any handouts used must be included in the video package. As with recording teacher performance, it is the planning for *use* which requires time and thought.

1.3 Production of Teacher Training Materials

The first use I discussed was that of recording teacher performance in order to provide feedback to the teachers recorded. Video recordings of classes can of course also be used to bring examples of classroom practice to trainees other than those recorded. In this case the camera's function is to take trainees into classrooms to observe selected aspects of what goes on—an invaluable extension of the trainee's experience. It is not, however, quite the same as sitting at the back of the class. The camera is selective, it does not look at the people and activities in a room in the same way as the human eye does. Additional explanation may therefore be necessary for an audience that was not involved in the actual class recorded and this can be added in various ways—by the tutor, in print, by video recording the teacher talking about the lesson.

Some institutions go so far as to produce on video self-standing teacher training programmes which combine extracts from classroom recordings with comment and explanation aimed at particular groups of teacher trainees. This kind of material requires careful planning, selection and editing and these production considerations are discussed later.

2. Uses in Direct Teaching

2.1 Recording Student Performance

The use of a video camera to provide a performer with a record of his/her performance applies to students as much as to teachers. Institutions use cameras to record various student activities: performance in oral tests, role plays, performance in simulated and real seminars, programmes devised and performed by students for other students. The recording is not technically difficult and indeed students can be involved behind the camera as well as in front of it.

Enrolment procedures often include interviews with students, as part of a test battery, and on some courses short test interviews are repeated at later stages. These oral tests are sometimes video recorded for later analysis or for use in orienting newcomers to the test procedures. The existence of such recordings offers the possibility of juxtaposing 'before and after' interviews in playback sessions with students to allow them to measure their own progress.

Many courses nowadays require students to participate in role-plays and simulations. Some teachers find that student motivation is increased when these are video recorded. It is also quite common for language programmes to include group tasks which require students to work together towards a given goal. When there is sufficient time available, for instance on an intensive course, the task of producing their own video programme is one which students find challenging and absorbing.

Students can gain a real sense of purpose from the knowledge that they are preparing and practising an activity for video recording. There is, too, the interest and satisfaction of seeing oneself in operation—particularly rewarding if the task being performed in the L_2 was previously beyond one's known capabilities. Video recording student performance enables teacher and students to recall the activity for a more considered and objective analysis than is possible during the event and they can focus not just on the words but also on all the non-verbal features which contribute to communication.

This new resource in the classroom can generate a great deal of enthusiasm but there is a danger that time is spent on making video recordings without there being a clear enough idea of the language learning purpose of the activity. Even when there are clearly defined objectives, there is still the problem of ensuring that feedback sessions are a worthwhile use of classroom time. If the purpose of recording students is to help them improve their performance in a foreign language then they have to have time to view the recording and they need to know what to look for and how to judge the results. Playback sessions take time and there is the additional problem that while students, like the rest of us, love to see themselves on the screen, they are not usually too interested in seeing the others perform. In some classrooms this problem can be minimized by organizing recording and playback sessions in small groups. In others viewing sessions are organized so that students are involved in assessing each other's performance[2].

2.2 Recording 'Raw' Data

The strength of video playback in a direct teaching programme must surely be its capacity to bring 'slices of life' into a classroom. With a video camera it is possible for teachers to record their own 'slices of life' as inputs to their own programmes. This can be done in a simple way, with the aim of letting students, via the camera, be 'flies on the wall' in a variety of situations. Depending on the language programme, institutions have used a video camera to collect examples of lectures and seminars, scientific and technical demonstrations, business and legal transactions and everyday practice in offices and the home. In the real situation students need to be able to use all available clues to help them interpret a situation; in the classroom an appropriate video recording can be used to help them prepare for the reality.

Again the actual recording can be done very simply: it is possible in some situations to set the camera so that the participants in the event are sensibly framed and then to lock the camera off—that is to leave it in a fixed position.

It then records the interaction that takes place, provided of course the participants do not all move to the other end of the room! In this way, students have the opportunity to 'sit in' on events such as the discussion of a contract, a salesman's visit, a transaction in a shop, an interview for a job or a family meal. Once the recording is obtained it is then a question of devising ways of helping students analyse and learn from the event as they observe it. Viewing guides which set specific tasks can provide a focus and group viewing with task sheets, followed by inter-group exchange of information is one possibility.

Once again it is planning for use, both before and after making the recording, that will determine whether the exercise is worthwhile.

2.3 Producing Specially Designed Teaching Material

It is of course also possible to script or otherwise structure video recording for a specific ELT purpose. The current gaps in published ELT video software and the proliferation of cameras in our lives encourage thoughts of home production and this possibility might be considered if the need for a video input to classroom activity has been identified and cannot be met from other sources. I am thinking here of programmes which are specially designed, with control over the content, as opposed to the recording of 'take what you get' raw data.

Specially designed material can take several forms. Colleagues and friends can be asked to perform certain activities in front of the camera; for example they may play a game, use a domestic appliance, interview each other or simply tell a story straight to camera. It is best if non-actors are not asked to act – self-consciousness shows up much more on video than on audio – but it is possible to set up natural-seeming activities which can be used in class for tasks such as note-taking or problem-solving. In some countries the injection of a local flavour by recording in a local setting with local people can be highly motivating. To attempt one's own production does of course raise the problem of identifying acceptable production standards and these are discussed in the following section.

3. Production Considerations

ELT practitioners are prolific producers: they run off their own worksheets, mount their own magazine pictures, invent their own games and audio record their own dialogues. When you give this do-it-yourself profession a do-it-yourself video camera it is not surprising to find that it generates great enthusiasm for home production. The problem is to channel that enthusiasm in sensible directions which take into account the kind of equipment, the level of training, the technical and production expertise and the amount of staff time the institution can afford. I have outlined six possible uses of video recording. Taking into account the time, expertise and equipment required, Figure 3 places these six uses on a simple-complex continuum.

Simple recording	Simple production		Complex production
Recording teacher/ student performance	Recording raw data/ institutional events/ classroom activities	Assemble editing from recordings of raw data/events/ classroom activity	Producing specially designed teaching or teacher training material

Figure 3. *Recording—Production: Simple—Complex.*

3.1 *Simple Recording*

I classify as simple recording the use of a video camera as a tool to enable teachers or students to view their own performance. I would expect this to be the primary use of a video camera in most ELT institutions, as it is in many other types of training. Simple recording requires the minimum of planning; the activity recorded does not need to be rehearsed or structured in any way for the camera; the equipment can be set up and operated by the teachers or students involved; the end result does not need to be edited. The time required to produce a simple recording is determined by the duration of the activity plus whatever time is needed to set up the equipment. Such a recording is normally viewed by those who were recorded and then it is erased, so it simply serves as a reminder of what took place and provides proof, if needed, of points under discussion. The technical quality is not therefore very important.

3.2 *Simple Production*

As soon as we move from recording for immediate feedback to the recording of material for an audience which did not participate in the recording, we are in the business of planning to get a message across to a particular audience. We need to take account of the knowledge, skills and experience that audience can draw on in viewing and interpreting the recording. We need to consider the effect the material will have on the teachers or students who will use it. This planning is the additional element which distinguishes production from straight recording and it applies even to the simple recording of a lecture, or of a 'fly on the wall' recording in a classroom.

The actual recording may still be of the simplest kind, but it needs to be planned in relation to the purpose for which it will be used. For example, lectures are sometimes video recorded for EAP programmes: if one sets out to record a real lecture, there are several questions to be answered regarding what will appear on the screen. Do we need to see the audience as well as the lecturer? Are we interested in what is written on the blackboard or only in how the lecturer introduces a new topic? If handouts are used, do we need to see one in close up? Does it matter if we cannot see (or hear) questioners in the audience? Is it essential to record the whole lecture and should the lecturer therefore be asked to pause for a change of tape? These questions can only be answered if those who asked for the recording have thought through why and how they will use it in the classroom.

The extent to which recordings will be used will also have a bearing on the form the end product will take. One tutor may select sequences from different classroom recordings as illustrations for one session with one group of teacher trainees. In this case it would be sufficient to have previewed the recordings and noted counter numbers so that the selected sequences can be found reasonably quickly in the training session. Any explanations about the context of the sequences can be given by the tutor who selected them. If, however, the tutor wishes to use the same selection with different groups at different times it is going to be more economic of time to edit those sequences on to one tape and it is very likely that a tutor who makes frequent use of the institution's own classroom recordings will eventually assemble a range of examples which can be grouped under different headings. It is also very likely that a collection like this will be of use to other tutors and should be available to them. Given library viewing facilities, the selections could also be made available to trainee teachers in a self access mode. Extended use of this kind calls for support material of some kind, to ensure that the context and the reason for making those particular selections remains clear to users who were not involved in making the selections.

Support may be provided by accompanying print or it may be built into the video tape by adding recordings of tutors or teachers commenting on the classroom extracts shown. In order to select from 'raw' recordings and to assemble these selections to make a programme it becomes necessary to have video editing facilities. This in turn implies the training of staff for video editing and the need for time to view, select and edit material, and to produce whatever support the programme needs to ensure effective use by others.

We are here moving into the realm of simple production as opposed to simple recording. It is possible to train interested teachers in short workshops to plan simple productions and to undertake basic camera operation and assemble editing. The problem is to decide, in relation to the needs and resources of an institution, just how much time can justifiably be spent on video production of this kind. A rule of thumb guide would be that simple production of the kind described should take an average of two to four hours planning and editing time on top of the time needed to set up and record.

However simple, production is time consuming. The results of simple, institutional production are not polished and would probably not travel outside the institution. There may well be a useful place in an institution for the production of simple teacher training programmes or of 'raw' data materials for direct teaching but the use and effectiveness of the results needs to be carefully monitored.

3.3 Complex Production

I have described uses of a video camera which require only simple recording techniques. I use the term 'complex production' in an institutional context for any production which attempts to do more than simply point a camera at an event as it happens. We may think that a documentary on TV is made by just letting the camera record a scene as it happens and indeed the sequence of images and sound are put together to give us that impression, but it *is* only a skilfully created impression. If a single camera is used, the same scene may be recorded three times from different angles and then edited so that, for instance, we see each person in close up when they talk. Recording in a studio with more than one camera is also quite complex, although in a different way, particularly if there is an attempt to suggest a setting other than a studio. It requires considerable skill, experience and a range of resources to plan and execute the production of a video sequence to convey the impression of a real, credible event.

Enthusiastic teachers often wish to attempt the production of 'slices of life' sequences but they do tend to underestimate the time and expertise required and to have unrealistic expectations of the small-format video equipment available to them and of the acting ability of their colleagues. It is one thing to use the camera as an unobtrusive observer of natural interaction—say a sales representative's interview with the school's administrator about a new book order—and quite another to try to create a similar scene using teacher colleagues as actors and scripting the interaction so as to control the language used. I suggest that the former comes within the confines of modest institutional production, whereas the end result of the latter is likely to be amateurish and unconvincing.

A production which has aims and content similar to published material has to have a certain professional polish if it is to be used at all extensively. It requires someone with production expertise, preferably combined with an ELT background, as well as staff who can give technical support; it requires editing equipment and a range of other resources and it will involve the producer and several others in a considerable expenditure of time. Some institutions are equipped and staffed to undertake production at this level but most are not. The latter, however, are often faced with the problem of attempting complex production without appreciating all that it involves. The checklist below attempts to provide them with some basic guidelines.

4. The Production Process: A Checklist

For simple or complex production, there are certain stages which need to be worked through to ensure that time and resources are used in a sensible, effective way. This checklist is designed for use in an institution to help those who have to make decisions about production proposals.

Stage One starts with **A Production Proposal**
Explore the ideas:
- Is there a need for this material?
- What is needed, why and for whom?
- Does something like it already exist?
- If it does not, or if you cannot get hold of it . . .

Explore production possibilities:
- Is there a case for in-house production?
- Is it within the capabilities of in-house resources?

Are the resources available?

may end with A Decision to Produce

Stage Two **Plan Production**
Specify objectives and target audience
Rcscarch and decide content
Plan total package (any accompanying print?)
Detailed planning for recording
- –recce locations
- –organize resources
- –produce schedule

Stage Three **Produce**
Record
Edit, if possible and necessary
Produce any supplementary material

Stage Four **Use and Evaluate**
Try out with target audience
Ensure potential users know about it
Order any copies needed
Catalogue in local system
Monitor frequency of use
Measure actual use against objectives
Consider need for revision/development

Conclusion

When a new technology is introduced to the classroom, there seems to be a tendency to concentrate on the technical 'how' rather than the pedagogic 'why'. Somehow the complexity of video technology leads people to suspend their normal critical thinking and one finds for instance that there is no training programme to introduce teachers to possible applications of the new resource or that there is no evaluation of the way it is being used. Perhaps it is just the thought of exploring a completely new area that discourages busy people but this does mean that video recording tends to become the preserve of a small band of enthusiasts. I am not suggesting that the enthusiasts should be discouraged, far from it, but rather that others profit from their enthusiasm by focusing on the results they produce.

It is sound pedagogic practice to measure actual use and actual results against intended use and results, and it is perfectly possible to do this without a detailed technical understanding of the resource. It is also sound practice for institutions thinking of acquiring a video camera to start by analysing possible applications in relation to the institution's own needs and resources before seeking technical advice.

Video technology is still developing rapidly and recording equipment is becoming lighter and easier to use but, however sophisticated the hardware becomes, it will only ever be as good as the results it helps the teacher and the learner achieve.

Notes and References

1. 'Video in English language: A guide to hardware options' in *Video in the language classroom*, Geddes and Sturtridge (eds), Heinemann Practical Language Teaching Series, 1981.
2. See 'Let Your Students Be Active: Using Videotape to Teach English as a Second Language' S. M. Griffin. *CATESOL. Occasional Papers No 3* (Winter 1976–77).

VIDEO IN ENGLISH FOR SPECIFIC PURPOSES

CHRIS KENNEDY

Introduction

The purpose of this paper is to review the developments taking place in the use of video in English for Specific Purposes (ESP) and suggest ways in which VTR/VCR equipment might enhance ESP teaching programmes. Although I shall make references to television and film, I shall assume that wherever possible TV programmes or films would be copied and used on video equipment, since a video unit, as well as being less cumbersome, provides the teacher with a flexibility that TV or film lack. A video tape can be stopped, wound forward, rewound, as the teacher and his students require, which gives the teacher control over the output of the programme. Lack of output control restricts a teacher's pedagogic moves and he cannot adjust and adapt his teaching to match learner-reaction to the material presented.

1. Type of Operation

There are always dangers that, like the language laboratory before it, video may be greeted as the panacea to ELT ills. This would be unfortunate. It is essential that video should be regarded as an aid that in certain circumstances with certain students can make the learning/teaching process more effective. We need to distinguish here between whole-job, major-job and minor-job operations (Pit Corder, 1966). A whole-job operation is one in which all the teaching is done through video. I do not intend to discuss the potential of this special type of operation for ESP here, although one could envisage programmes for example for businessmen needing the language skills required for business and social transactions conducted in English.

In the major-job operation, video is used as a support for inadequately-trained teachers or teachers with a weak command of the language, presenting material which they would be unable to teach themselves. This approach could be useful in ESP programmes, with video programmes not only supplementing a teacher's lack of linguistic skills but also his lack of knowledge of the content area, as both native and non-native teachers often feel insecure when teaching from scientific and technical texts. However, the cost effectiveness of this type of operation must be realistically assessed. The money spent in video production of this sort might be better spent providing the teacher with more in-service training, more textbooks and relatively cheap aids such as tape recorders. We have to take a hard-headed look at why we use video at all. It must do something the teacher cannot do or does poorly. It must be regarded as an aid to a teaching programme, not as an independent programme in itself, and its use should be carefully integrated with other materials used on a course (Cleary, 1978; Brock, 1979; Hansen, 1979). These criteria point to the minor-job operation in which video is used with experienced, trained teachers as a teaching device in the context of a full programme of course work.

2. ESP and Video

Looking at ELT in terms of ESP has certain implications for methodology and materials and so for the use of video in an ESP programme. Underlying much ESP work is a concern with the development in the learner of varying stages of communicative competence and of the teaching of language as a system of communication. This implies that learning will be focused to an increasing extent on a view of language as *use*, on communicative abilities as well as linguistic skills. We have to go further, however, to discover which communicative abilities and what aspects of them are required by the learner in the 'real-life' situations for which he is being trained by the language teacher. So that materials should reflect the learner's needs as closely as possible, the learner's terminal goals are taken as course aims and serve as input to the design of thc materials which are therefore often based on 'authentic' data. The success of the ESP programme will then be measured by the ability of the learner to perform in the 'real-life' situation, which might be reading an engineering journal article, listening to a lecture on sociology, or participating in an academic seminar. However relevant the materials, they will not succeed unless in addition they both motivate the learner because of their liveliness and interest and also demand his actual participation and involvement in some way.

Taking these socio-psycholinguistic considerations into account, we can begin to see the advantages of exploiting video in ESP teaching. Video is highly motivating for the learner. It can expose him to 'live' instances of communication rather than the usual simulations which teachers or textbook writers have to resort to. It can show him the situations in which he will have to operate, can present examples of successful and unsuccessful interaction, and more important can show why misunderstandings might occur and how to avoid breakdowns in communication. The learner's terminal behaviour can be brought into the classroom rather than exist as an abstract ideal outside it. At the same time, because of the control the teacher has over output, both teacher and learner have time and opportunities to select and discuss those aspects of the materials which need clarification or explanation.

3. Video and Skills Development

I should now like to look at various skills to see to what extent video can contribute to developing them. Although for organizational reasons I shall be writing about isolated skills, I hope it will become clear that I advocate an integrated approach to skills teaching. I should also point out that the examples given are of work done with overseas students in Britain as they are the type of EFL learner with whom Birmingham University's English Department has most contact.

3.1 Reading and Writing

It is difficult to see how video could be used to improve a learner's ability to read and write which a textbook could not do as well or better. The training of these two abilities involves exposure to large units of discourse in texts and practice in decoding and encoding their rhetorical structure. Video cannot provide exposure of this sort to a large body of text. However, the more 'mechanical' reading skills such as those mentioned by Ewer may be trained using video. Many non-native readers have difficulty in hand manipulation and left-to-right eye movement in the early stages of reading and writing and Sherrington (1973) has suggested techniques for training these skills. Roller captions can be used to increase reading speed and the ability to skim and scan for information. Sub-titles used with a visual presentation are compulsive reading and this is a further technique which could be exploited for training reading skills. Elementary composing and comprehending exercises, training the learner to recognize and copy letters, words and structures could also be visually presented.

Note-taking is a particular study skill which many overseas students have difficulty with in the course of their studies at English-medium colleges and universities. Here video can be used to present a stimulus, in the form of a description of a process, an account of an experiment, or a lecture, to which the student responds by taking notes. Notice that the role of video here is not to teach note-taking skills as such, but to present a realistic verbal and non-verbal context in which the activity of note-taking may take place. Bearing in mind what was said above about an integrative methodology for teaching skills, a learning cycle might take the following form:

(i) listening to/watching a video-taped lecture/talk
(ii) at the same time taking notes or
(iii) completing various note-taking exercises
(iv) follow-up discussion of the notes in pairs/groups
(v) possible writing-up of notes into a full report.

This integrated approach is followed by Geddes (1976) in her teaching materials which illustrate the integration of video in a learning/teaching sequence exploiting various skills at different times within the teaching unit. A topic is selected for the unit e.g. Rural Urban Migration. The students approach the topic through introductory readings, then listen to/watch a video-taped lecturette and take notes. Further reading follows and the information the students have gained as a result of their reading/listening/note-taking is then exploited in a seminar-type discussion. Starkey (1978) suggests a similar integrated methodology, using technical films for listening, note-taking, writing and discussion. Note that these programmes involve the student in active participation—the value of video is lessened if active student response is not built into the materials.

3.2 Listening

In talking of note-taking skills I have already introduced the topic of listening. One of the major advantages of video in ESP is that it can present to a learner A-V recordings of the academic situation he will be faced with in his role as a student following a particular subject speciality, engineering, physics, etc. Sturtridge *et al.* (1977) use video-taped lecturettes for extensive listening and intensive analysis during which they focus attention on '. . . the organization of discourse, including markers of enumeration, exemplification, parenthesis, hesitation, digression, self-correction, and repetition; . . . the content of the lecturette; . . . the students' notes as a reflection of its content and its organization . . .' (p. 110). They report that the addition of the visual and non-verbal features of discourse made available through video makes the lecturettes easier to understand than those recorded on audio tape alone. This we would expect as by denying a learner access to the non-verbal features of discourse we are removing a valuable aid to understanding which is present in normal face-to-face interaction. (Beattie, 1977).

Video can also present information visually which would normally only be accessible in written form or through 'stills', for example, an industrial process or heavy industrial or scientific equipment. In cases such as this both language and science content can be presented and explicated together. Adams-Smith (1978) uses film for team-teaching sessions between language teachers and subject specialists, a welcome move towards integration of language and content. During the first showing of the film, language points are raised and clarified by the language teacher; during a second showing, a subject specialist joins the group and discusses its content with the students, answering their technical rather than linguistic questions.

3.3 Speaking

Since a video recording is able to present authentic situations and show individuals interacting with each other, it might be thought that its main use could be in developing oral skills. However, its use in practising oral skills is at the moment limited, since although video can present two-way communication, a viewer cannot practise interaction with screen characters. Video participation as we have seen in the sections on note-taking and listening, tends to take the form of non-reciprocal activity, whereas the essence of the spoken mode is that it is a reciprocal social activity, which can be shown to viewers but without their 'on-line' participation (Sherrington, 1973).

Knight (1975) reports the successful use of video in a course in spoken

English at tertiary level. He comments on the motivating power of video and improvement in learning and retention: '. . . It has been noticeable here how very well students remember language and behaviour when it is presented in a life-like video programme . . .' (p. 82). In the programme described, 2–5 minute films are produced using local facilities which show English in use in certain situations and which are then developed for role-play purposes. Although it is accepted that 'social' English should play a part in an ESP programme and a number of projects exist for developing the oral skills of overseas students in the social situations they will meet inside and outside university, video recordings have up to now not been included as part of the course designs. This is regrettable since video could play a valuable role in helping an overseas student overcome communication difficulties with landlords/police/travel agents/booking clerks/lecturers/fellow students.

Research also indicates that many overseas students experience great difficulties in seminars. Materials such as those described by Johns and Johns (1978) could be usefully supplemented by illustrations of seminars and both successful and unsuccessful examples of communication. At the moment it is the linguistic aspects of seminar interaction which are most easily taught, but as more information is gathered about non-verbal cues exploited in spoken discourse, so video will be able to illustrate their use. We already know the importance of eye-contact in communication: 'During social interaction, people look each other in the eye, repeatedly but for short periods . . .. Without eye contact, people do not feel that they are fully in communication . . ..' (Argyle and Dean, 1972, p. 301). A survey by Sinclair Rogers (1977) confirmed the existence of difficulties overseas students have in spoken interaction. Problems included their reluctance or inability to take an active part in discussions, difficulty in opening and closing conversations and changing topic, and not understanding the visual signals of non-verbal communication. Rogers has an interesting approach to these problems. He organizes video workshops in which the students study illustrations of verbal and non-verbal aspects of communication and discuss examples of successful or failed communication. Short television documentaries are also produced by the students themselves on problems experienced by overseas students or on topics related to their subject area. There are great advantages in approaching the teaching of communication skills in this way. The students are on the one hand being trained to analyse discourse in a non-technical but highly relevant way and at the same time are using language and expressing themselves in very real situations.

This process of participation by the learner in his own learning situation is emphasized in the materials and methodology of the Lancaster Study Skills Programme (Candlin *et al.*, 1978) which attempts to train overseas students in self-evaluation and analysis of their performance and others' in seminars. Videos of overseas students interacting in seminars are shown to the course participants and discussed by them. The participants then prepare reading passages and note discussion points which they wish to raise and discuss in a subsequent TV tutorial with their subject tutors. I should point out that these three phases are just part of an integrated programme of listening to lectures, reading comprehension and language laboratory pairwork, and so do not exist independently from the study skills package but form an integral part of it.

4. Self-Access Materials

So far in this paper, I have assumed that video would be an aid to the 'normal' situation of learner-centred but teacher-directed operations. However with the advent of video-cassette recorders, which are reliable, compact and simple to operate, a potential for video in the development of self-access materials appears very real. A language laboratory filled with VCR equipment is expensive now, but as VCR production increases, no doubt costs will no longer be so prohibitive. Listening comprehension materials could benefit enormously from the addition of a visual element and one of the problems associated with language laboratory materials, namely that they can be boring and de-motivating, might well be overcome or at least considerably alleviated by the introduction of VCR equipment.

5. Research

I have been painting an optimistic picture of the use of video in ESP programmes. Interested and motivated teachers are developing techniques and materials using VCR/VTR equipment in their particular situation for the needs of their students. In the field, then, things look reasonably healthy. However, there is little research being conducted into video and its application (the Aston Video Research Group being an exception). We need to know more accurately where in a teaching programme video is most useful and what particular skills it can foster; what techniques and methods are most efficient; which learners benefit most from video and what problems/advantages video presents for them; what demands video places on the teacher; whether groups taught through video show improvements that other groups do not—these are basic questions and we need to find out the answers to these and many other questions if video is to become a valid, efficient component in ESP programmes.

6. Constraints

VCR/VTR equipment is costly and mechanically complex. Before embarking on programmes involving video, certain conditions should be satisfied. The most important are:

(a) Facilities and personnel must exist for maintenance and repair of equipment.
(b) Facilities must exist for making and showing programmes.
(c) If a TV/video unit is to be responsible for the technical production of programmes, the technical personnel must be willing and able to co-operate with the teachers in a team effort—technician and teacher

should be prepared to learn from one another and understand each other's problems.

(d) Teachers must be trained in the use of video equipment, or should be willing to be trained, should be willing to make programmes themselves, and be able to exploit video as a teaching aid, not as a substitute for the teacher.

(e) There should be a use for video which arises from the needs of the learners and the syllabus and materials based on those needs.

Summary

I hope I have shown that, wisely used, video can enhance ESP teaching programmes. It should not be regarded as a substitute for the teacher but as an important aid to the teaching. As such, it should be used as a component of an integrated skills package. To be handled effectively, it needs trained teachers and this implies teacher-training courses in the mechanics and methodology of video (Kennedy, 1978). Materials should be designed so that students can actively participate in and respond to video recordings. 'On-line' participation is difficult to achieve, especially in the teaching of oral skills since video is limited to presenting aspects of communication. Varied and motivating exercises designed to develop 'off-line' participation therefore need to be developed. More basic research is needed so that teachers can confidently use video at maximum efficiency.

The advantages of video are that it offers the teacher a flexible teaching instrument which can record interaction for replay and feedback; it can present 'authentic' data, show language in use in a variety of situations and demonstrate the inter-play of verbal and non-verbal aspects of discourse; it provides a means of presenting to the learner, for analysis and discussion, instances of his own and others' behaviour in relevant interactions; it can demonstrate processes or equipment which are not accessible to the learner in the classroom or in the laboratory; finally, evidence indicates that video is motivating for the learner, increases retention of material and, by providing visual support, aids comprehension of spoken discourse.

We have seen that in an ESP situation, video is particularly useful in developing study skills such as note-taking, listening to lectures and participating in seminars and that it has great potential as a valuable aid in both academic and social life.

References

ADAM-SMITH, D. (1978) 'Co-operative teaching: bridging the gap between E and SP', in *Al Manakh*, **2**, (2) University of Kuwait Language Centre.

ARGYLE, M. and DEAN, J. (1972) 'Eye Contact, Distance and Application', in Laver and Hutchinson (eds) *Communication in Face to Face Interaction*, Penguin.

BEATTIE, N. (1977) Non-Verbal Aspects of the Teaching and Learning of Foreign Languages, *Audio Visual Language Journal*, **XV**:2.

BROCK, B. (1979) 'The Science Film in the English Classroom', *EST Newsletter* No 24.
CANDLIN, C. N. *et al.* (1978) 'Study Skills in English: theoretical issues and practical problems' in Mackay and Mountford (eds) *English for Specific Purposes*, Longman.
CLEARY, J. (1978) 'The Use of Video-Tape Recordings on the Communication Skills in English Project', ELT Documents *English for Specific Purposes.*
EWER, J., *Preparing Speed-Reading Materials for EST*, University of Chile (undated mimeo).
GEDDES, M. (1976) *ELTI Notes Video 21*, British Council.
HANSEN, A. (1979) 'Suggestions for VTR Lessons in EST', *EST Newsletter* No 24.
JOHNS, C. and JOHNS, T. (1977) 'Seminar Discussion Strategies', in Cowie and Heaton (eds) *English for Academic Purposes*, BAAL.
KENNEDY, C. J. (1978) 'A video course for teachers', *System*, **6** (3).
KNIGHT, M. (1975) 'Video in oral proficiency training', *System*, **3** (2).
PIT CORDER, S. (1966) 'Modern Foreign Language Teaching by Television', in Valdman (ed) *Trends in Language Teaching*, McGraw-Hill.
ROGERS, S. (1977) 'The Communicative Needs of Some Overseas Post-Graduate Students', in Cowie and Heaton (eds) *English for Academic Purposes*, BAAL.
SHERRINGTON, R. (1976) *Television and Language Skills*, OUP.
STARKEY, B. (1978) 'The Use of Technical Films in English', *Al Manakh*, **1** (1).
STURTRIDGE, E. *et al.* (1977) 'The British Council and the English Language Problems of Overseas Students', in Cowie and Heaton (eds) *English for Academic Purposes*, BAAL.

THE USE OF VIDEO IN ENGLISH LANGUAGE TEACHING

BIBLIOGRAPHY

ADAM-SMITH, D. (1978) Cooperative teaching: bridging the gap between E and SP. *Al-Manakh* (Kuwait), **2,** (2) 15–18.

AK-GAYLANI, G. (1979) Film—a medium for language teaching. *IDELTI Bulletin*, No. 7. 5–8. (EFL in Iraq).

AL-HAMASH, K. L. (1978) The role of educational television in the teaching of English in Iraq. *IDELTI Bulletin*, No. 3. 5–6.

ATIENZA, L. J. (1977) VTR workshop: small format video. Paris: Unesco, (Distributed by Centre for Advanced TV Studies, London). (A practical introduction to small scale video production which assumes no prior technical knowledge.)

BAER, E. R. (ed.) (1976) Teaching languages: ideas and guidance for teachers working with adults. British Broadcasting Corporation. (Includes the chapter: Making the most of radio and television.)

BARLENBACH, I. F. (1978) Video tape as an instructional aid in teaching German grammar. *NALLD Journal USA*, **12,** (2) 21–24.

BESSIERE, L. (1977) For a multi-media approach to language teaching. *Australian Review of Applied Linguistics*, **1,** (1) 57–61.

BRIGHTON POLYTECHNIC (1980) Language Teaching Research Unit. The use of radio and television language programmes. Falmer, Sussex: Brighton Polytechnic Language Centre. (Typescript of paper presented to the CEREB Conference. Includes surveys of users of BBC *Kontakte* and *Le Nouvel arrive* courses.)

BRINTON, D. and GASKILL, W. (1978) Using new broadcasts in the ESL/EFL classroom. *TESOL Quarterly* (USA) **12,** (4) 403–413.

BRITISH BROADCASTING CORPORATION (1977) An introduction to further education broadcasts. London: BBC. (A guide for teachers including details of policy and copyright restrictions.)

BRITISH BROADCASTING CORPORATION (1980) Learning languages from the BBC: research into courses, by Stephanie Rybak. London: BBC. (Reports on user surveys covering BBC adult-education courses for French, German, Spanish and Russian and on support schemes.)

BRITISH BROADCASTING CORPORATION (1978) Parosi: a BBC contribution to language learning in the Asian community, by Tony Matthews. London: BBC. (Describes the production of a television series and the support activities accompanying it. The series is intended to encourage non-English-speaking Asians living in Britain, especially women, to learn English.)

BRITISH BROADCASTING CORPORATION (1981) (English by Radio and Television). Using video in the classroom. London: BBC English by Radio and Television. (A short booklet with ideas on the use of video illustrated by specific examples from BBC EFL programmes.)

BROUGHTON, G. (1971) Language teaching by film. *Educational Media International*, (4) 12–15.

CALSOYAS, K. A. and CALSOYAS, J. A. (1981) Television in the classroom. *English Teaching Forum* (USA), **19,** (4). 2–4.

CANDLIN, J., CHARLES, D. and WILLIS, J. (1982) 'Video in English Language Teaching', University of Aston in Birmingham, *Language Studies Unit Research Report*.

CASLER, K. (1980) Video materials in language learning. *Modern English Teacher*, **8,** (2) 16–22.

CLAUSING, G. *et al.* (1974) The contribution of television in media-aided programs. *NALLD Journal* (USA), **8**, (2) 19–32. (Describes the integration of television into German teaching at the University of Minnesota.)

CLEARY, J. (1978) The use of video tape recordings on the Communication Skills in English Project, K.A.A.U. In: *English for specific purposes*. pp. 76–80. London: British Council (ELT documents, 101).

CORDER, S. Pit (1966) *The Visual Element in Language Teaching*. London: Longman.

COUNCIL OF EUROPE (1972) Committee for General and Technical Education. The teaching of modern languages by closed circuit television and other audio-visual media. Report of the Meeting of Experts, Glasgow. Strasbourg: Council of Europe, 172. 44p.

COUNCIL OF EUROPE (1970) Council for Cultural Co-operation. The reception of and response to modern language teaching programmes by television intended for the general public, by Wolfgang Halm. Strasbourg: Council of Europe. (Includes brief details of broadcasts in most Western European countries and an analysis of the survey.)

CRABB, G. (1976) Copyright clearance: a practical guide. London: Council for Educational Technology.

CROUSE, G. and NOLL, B. A. (1980) Using videotape to teach foreign languages. *Foreign Language Annals* (USA), **13**, (5) 391–393.

DAM JENSEN, E. and VINTHER, T. (1978) Video in foreign language teaching, *System*, **6**, (1) 25–29.

DAS, B. K. (1975) Educational television in the India context—a language teacher's point of view. *CIEFL Bulletin* (Hyderabad), **11**, 73–82. Language Teaching and Linguistics: Abstracts 1976–296.

DUKE, J. (1980) How not to use the video. *Modern English Teacher*, **8**, (2) 14–15.

ECKLUND, C. L. and WEISE, P. (1981) French accent through video analysis. *Foreign Language Annals* (USA), **14**, (1) 17–23.

ELT DOCUMENTS, 105 (1979) The use of the media in English language teaching. London: The British Council, English Teaching Information Centre. (Contains articles on the use of radio and television in teaching English to non-native speakers.)

FORMANEK, M. (1974) The contribution of television in media-aided language programs. (German language program—University of Minnesota). *NALLD Journal* (USA), **8**, (2) 19–32.

FOSS, H. (ed.) (1980–) Video production techniques: a handbook for television, film and audio-visual program makers. London: Kluwer. (Loose leaf publication). An authoritative guide to video production.

FRIEDMAN, E. (1979) English by television and foreign language learning. Tel Aviv: Centre for Educational Technology (for the) Instructional Television Center, Ministry of Education and Culture. (A guide to the use of television in Israel with extensive illustrations and appendices relating to specific programmes.)

GEDDES, M. and STURTRIDGE, G. (1981) *Video in the Language Classroom*. London: Allen & Unwin. (Practical language teaching, 7).

GEORGE, S. E. (1980) Language is not a sterile void!: from video-tape to role play: an advanced course of oral interaction. *Papers on Work in Progress* (Italy); (3). 5–11.

GOLDBERG, M. (1976) Accessible portapak manual. Vancouver, B.C.: Satellite Video Exchange Society (distributed in the UK by the Centre for Advanced TV Studies, 42 Theobald's Road, London WC1). (A comprehensive and comprehensible portapak manual for small format video practitioners.)

GOODSON, W. (1978) Techniques for the use of films in language teaching. *Language Reporter* (Malaysia) **6**, (14) 5–8.

GOVIER, R. A. (ed.) (1976) *Films and How to Use Them: a Handbook for the Foreign Language Teacher*, Philadelphia, Pa.: National Carl Schurz Association.

GREENE, J. (1979) Live from the language lab: conversation classes on TV. *Canadian Modern Languages Review*. **35**, (4) 621–624.

GRIFFIN, S. M. (1980) Video studios: the language labs for the 1980s. *Cross Currents* (Japan), **7**, (1) 45–58.

HAMBROOK, J. (1979) English by television: recent developments. *Educational Broadcasting International*. **12**, (3) 140–141.

HENDERSON, J. and HUMPHRIES, F. (eds) (1981) Audio visual handbook: the SCET guide to educational and training equipment. London: Kogan Page. Replaces Sections 2 and 3 of the *NAVAC audio visual handbook* (see under NATIONAL AUDIO VISUAL AIDS CENTRE).

HILL, B. (1981) Some applications of media technology to the teaching and learning of languages. *Language Teaching and Linguistics: Abstracts*, **14**, (3) 147–161. (Survey article covering broadcast media. Includes bibliography.)

HILL, B. and BARLEY, A. (1977) Using language broadcasts. *Audio-Visual Language Journal*, **15**, (1) 54–60. Language Teaching & Linguistics: Abstracts 1978–304.

HILL, J. K. (1978) The recording and use of off-air French television programmes with advanced language learners. *Audio-Visual Language Journal*, **16**, (2) 81–84.

HODAPP, T. (1978) Video as an instructional aid for English as a second language teaching. *Research in the Teaching of English* (USA), **12**, (2) 163–167.

HUTCHINGS, P. (1979) Making the most of the news. *Times Educational Supplement*, 16 November. Modern Language Teaching Extra p. 39. News in French/German on BBC Television.

KANABA, S. (1980) The roles of U-matic vs. VHS: consideration for educational technologists. *NALLD Journal* (USA), **14**, (3/4) 5–8.

KEARNEY, M.-L. (1981) The role of video in auto-correction. *Creativity*, (Sao Paulo) (38). 1–4.

KEILSTRUP, D. V. (1980) Using the situation-oriented miniplay and the videotape recorder in advanced conversation classes. *Foreign Language Annals* (USA), **13**, (5) 367–370.

KENNEDY, C. (1978) A video course for teachers. *System*, **6**, (3) 139–143.

KENNEDY, C. (1979) Video in ESP. *Journal of English Language Teaching* (India), **14**, (6) 199–210.

KNIGHT, M. (1975) Video and oral proficiency training. *System*, **3**, (2) 81–83.

LALLY, D. V. (1971) Video tape recorders and the foreign language teacher. *NALLD Journal* (USA), **6**, (2) 22–26.

LAW, M. (1980) How television can help the modern language teacher. *British Journal of Language Teaching*, **18**, (2/3) 120–128. (Examples from Thames Television's French programmes.)

McINNES, J. (1981) *Video in education and training*. London: Focal Press. (This handbook gives working methods for a variety of simple but effective techniques, showing the importance of ingenuity over lavish budget.)

MACKNIGHT, F. R. (1981) Review and analysis of present video use in E.F.L. teaching. M.Ed. dissertation, University College, Cardiff.

McLEAN, A. (1975) New roles for television in the teaching of English to immigrant children. *System*, **3**, (3) 185–189. *Language Teaching & Linguistics: Abstracts* 1976–128.

McLEAN, A. (1976) TV comedy and the teaching of English. *English Language Teaching Journal*, **31**, (1) 10–16.

McLEAN, A. (1975) The uses of follow-up: television in the classroom. *English Language Teaching Journal*, **29**, (4) 303–309. *Language Teaching & Linguistics: Abstracts* 1976–59.

MASTERMAN, L. (1980) *Teaching About Television*. London: Macmillan.

MODERN ENGLISH TEACHER (1979) **7**, (2). Special issue: Focus on using the media.

NATIONAL AUDIO VISUAL AIDS CENTRE (1980) *NAVAC audio visual handbook*. London: Kogan Page. Sections 2 and 3 have been replaced by the new (SCET) edition (see under HENDERSON, J. and HUMPHRIES, F. eds.) but Section 1, especially the article 'Choosing and using video equipment', remains useful.

NORMAND, G. (1980) Motivating with media: the use of video at the elementary and intermediate level in high school and college. *Canadian Modern Language Review*, **37**, (1) 51–56. (Includes bibliography.)

ODOM, W. (1976) The use of videotape in foreign language instruction: a survey. *NALLD Journal* (USA), **10**, (3/4).

OZETTE, O. *et al.* (1976) Two facets of our instructional television production 'Asi se hace el vino'. *NALLD Journal* (USA), **11**, (1) 7–16. (Describes the pedagogical and practical points to be considered in video production.)

PARKER, D. V. (1976) Adapting the commercial feature film to the ESOL student. *English*

Language Teaching Journal, **31,** (1) 24–29. *Language Teaching & Linguistics: Abstracts* 1977–271.

PIERCY, M. (1977) Using BBC 'Voix de France' with 1st year A-level pupils. *Audio-Visual Language Journal*, **15,** (1) 60–64.

REISH, J. G. and RÉISH, H. K. (1980) The preparation and classroom use of a videotaped play: Ionesco's 'La Leçon'. *Canadian Modern Language Review*, **36,** (2) 257–265.

RIETMANN, K. (1981) Adding sight and sound to computer assisted instruction: interactive video. *English for Specific Purposes* (Oregon), Issue 53, pp. 3 and 5.

RILEY, P. and ZOPPIS, C. (1976) The sound and video library: an interim report on an experiment. *Melánges Pedágogiques.* 125–143. Reprinted in Dirven, R. (ed.) (1977) *Horverstandnis im Fremdsprachenunterricht.* pp. 155–168. Kronenberg: Scriptor.

RILEY, P. (1981) Viewing comprehension 'l'oeil ecoute'. In: *The Teaching of Listening Comprehension: (Papers presented at the Goethe-Institut Colloquium held in Paris in 1979).* London: British Council. (ELT documents. Special).

ROBERTSON, A. (ed.) (1981) *International Video Yearbook 1981.* Poole, Dorset: Blandford Press. A comprehensive directory of video equipment and services. This 5th edition has international coverage.)

ROMISZOWSKI, A. J. (1974) *The Selection and Use of Instructional Media.* Rev. edn. London: Kogan Page. (Shows how an analysis of the instructional problem can be made before matching needs with particular media.)

ROWATT, R. W. (1980) *Video: a Guide to the Use of Portable Video Equipment.* Glasgow: Scottish Council for Educational Technology. (An outline guide to equipment needed to make your own recordings.)

SCHOOL BROADCASTING COUNCIL FOR THE UNITED KINGDOM (1977) *An Introduction to School Broadcasts.* Rev. edn. London: British Broadcasting Corporation (for) SBC. (A guide for teachers to BBC schools broadcasts policy and arrangements, including the distribution of support material and copyright restrictions.)

SEMINAR ON VIDEO APPLICATIONS IN ENGLISH LANGUAGE TEACHING (1979) Video applications in English language teaching: report of the seminar held at the British Council's Language Teaching Institute, London, 3–5 January 1979. London: ELTI.

SHEERIN, S. Exploiting an off-air video: some considerations and a case study, In: *Lexden Papers 1: essays on teaching English for specific purposes.* Colchester (19 Lexden Road, Colchester, Essex): Lexden Centre.

SHERRINGTON, R. (1973) *Television and Language Skills.* Oxford University Press. (Examines the potential of television for language learning from linguistic and pedagogical standpoints.)

SKIRBLE, R. (1979) 'Let your TV do the talking'—using the VTR in the EFL Classroom. *Cross Currents* (Japan), **6,** (2) 37–46.

STURTRIDGE, G., McALPIN, J. and HARPER, D. (1977) The British Council and the English language problems of overseas students: English for academic purposes materials development. In: *English for Academic Purposes: Papers on the Language Problems of Overseas Students in Higher Education in the UK*, A. P. Cowie and J. B. Heaton (eds). Reading: British Association for Applied Linguistics (SELMOUS/BAAL Seminar).

SWAIN, D. V. (1981) *Scripting for Video and Audiovisual Media.* London: Focal Press. (Draws on wide-ranging examples to demonstrate the script's role in communicating concepts, simplifying production and cutting costs.)

TAGGART, G. and MOORE, G. A. B. (1972) The use of closed-circuit television for oral tests in the language laboratory. *NALLD Journal* (USA), **7,** (1) 27–30.

TASSICKER, M. (1981) Using TV for teaching ESL to adults. *TEFL/TESL Newsletter* (Australia), **5,** (4) 39–46.

THOMAS, J. P. (1980) Close encounters—of four kinds: the development of BBC Schools Television language broadcasts. *British Journal of Language Teaching*, **18,** (2/3) 107–113. French and German series.

VERNON, P. J. (ed.) (1973) *The Audio-Visual Approach to Modern Language Teaching: a Symposium.* London: National Audio-Visual Aids Centre (distributor). (Includes articles on the use of films as background material and on the use of radio and television.)

WEGNER, H. (1977) *Feature Films in Second Language Instruction.* Arlington, Va: Center for Applied Linguistics, ERIC Clearinghouse on Languages and Linguistics. (Includes a description of how written and audio material can be prepared for use with commercial feature films in the language classroom.)

WILLIAMS, F. and VAN WART, G. (1974) *Carrascolendas: Bilingual Education Through Television*. New York: Praeger. (Gives details of the impact of a successful bilingual education, Spanish, English, television programme for children in the United States.)

RESOURCES

BRITISH BROADCASTING CORPORATION (1981) BBC Enterprises film and video catalogue. London: BBC Enterprises. Lists films and video cassettes available for hire and purchase. Includes some language courses (not EFL).

BRITISH BROADCASTING CORPORATION (1981) English by Radio and Television BBC English courses 1981 (broadsheet). London: BBC English by Radio and Television. General leaflet covering BBC English courses with a price list (UK) which gives details of books and audio-recordings. Includes a timetable of BBC English by radio broadcasts and a list of overseas agents. (Supplement: New BBC English courses 80/81).

BRITISH BROADCASTING CORPORATION (1981) English by Radio and Television BBC English-teaching film, video and multi-media courses for broadcasting and institutional use 1981/2. London: BBC English by Radio and Television.

THE BRITISH COUNCIL (1980) English Language Division *and* Central Information Service. Audio visual aids to English language teaching. London: British Council. (ETIC information guide 4). Includes annotated lists of films for ELT and training of language teachers. Also lists other formats.

MARY GLASGOW PUBLICATIONS. Films for language teaching: film and video programmes in English, French and German. Kineton: Mary Glasgow Publications. Lists films/video-cassettes and supporting materials.

THOMAS NELSON & SONS. Nelson Filmscan programmes. Walton-on-Thames: Nelson Filmscan, (forthcoming). Film and video materials with accompanying books and audio-cassettes for EFL and ESP.

JOURNALS OF INTEREST

BBC London Calling, BBC External Service, Bush House, London. Monthly.

British Journal of Educational Technology, Councils and Education Press, London. 3 issues per year.

British Journal of Language Teaching (formerly *Audio-Visual Language Journal*), Published by the British Association for Language Teaching. Available from Mrs E. A. Dyson, Glan Ffrwd, Fernbrook Road, Penmaenmawr, Gwynedd. LL34 6DE. 3 issues per year.

Educational Broadcasting International, Published for the British Council by Peter Peregrinus Ltd, Hitchin, Herts.

English Language Teaching Journal, Published by Oxford University Press in association with the British Council. 4 issues per year.

ESL Video Newsletter, World English Centre, University of San Francisco. To be replaced by *Language Video International.*

Journal of the Centre for Advanced TV Studies. (International Review of Video and Mass Media). CATS, 42 Theobalds Road, London. WC1Z 8NW. 2 issues per year. Gives summary abstracts of important articles.

Journal of Educational Television and Other Media, Educational Television Association, 86 Micklegate, York. YO1 1JZ. 3 issues per year.

Modern English International (succeeds *BBC Modern English*), Modern English International, 8 Hainton Avenue, Grimsby, South Humberside. DN32 9BB.

NALLD Journal, (National Association of Learning Laboratory Directors). Academic Publications, University of Louisville, Kentucky, USA. 3 issues per year.

System, International Journal of Educational Technology and Language Learning Systems. Pergamon Press, Oxford. 3 issues per year.

World Language English, The International Teachers' Journal of English as a World Language. Pergamon Press, Oxford. 4 issues per year.

Compiled by John Hawkins, Assistant Librarian, Language Teaching Library, with contributions from Pru Watts-Russell, Librarian, British Council Media Department.

ABOUT THE AUTHORS

Margaret Allen spent several years teaching and developing audio materials in the British Council's English Language Teaching Institute, London before training in the production of educational film and television. She then went to Iran, as the Council's Educational Technology Officer from 1974 to 1978 and now heads its Audio Visual Unit in London. She has run courses in the applications of video in ELT in several of the Council's Language Centres overseas and she is at present producing a series of ELT materials under the general title *Classroom Video*. She is also responsible for the production of the video component of a teacher training package currently being developed by the Council's English Language Services Department. She has a degree in Modern Languages and a Diploma in Education from the University of Edinburgh and trained as a teacher at Moray House College of Education.

Chris Kennedy is Lecturer in Applied Linguistics in the English Department at the University of Birmingham, with responsibility for teacher-training courses. He has taught and lectured in West Africa, the Far East, the Middle East, South Africa and Europe. His areas of interest are teacher-training, language planning and language across the curriculum. He is founder and editor of *English Language Research Journal.*

Jack Lonergan is a freelance author and teacher trainer working from London. After taking an MEd in TEO at Manchester University in 1975, he set up the English Teaching Resources Centre in Wuppertal for the Centre for British Teachers. From 1978 to 1980 he directed a federal teacher training project for teachers of English in adult education institutes working with the multi-media course *Follow Me*, being based at the Pädagogische Arbeitsstelle des Deutschen Volkshochschul-Verbandes in Frankfurt. He has lectured throughout Europe, and published numerous articles on teacher training and methodology.

Frances MacKnight has worked as a teacher of English as a native, second and foreign language in Britain. She has also worked as an EFL teacher in Italy, Turkey and Iran. Recently she completed an MEd in TEFL and the subject of her dissertation was video use in EFL teaching in the UK.

John McGovern is a British Council officer who recently took up the post of Assistant Representative in Jordan. Since 1979 he has worked in English Language Services Department in London and been involved in the design and trialling of video materials. Prior to joining the Council he worked as an ESL/GFL teacher in Greece, Britain and Iran.

Dave Willis worked as a teacher of English in Ghana and Cyprus before joining the British Council. As Director of Studies in Tehran, he was responsible for designing a course for beginners which integrated the use of video. He is currently completing a PhD, the subject of which is Discourse Analysis and Syllabus Design, and will shortly be going to Singapore to take up the post of English Language Officer.

Jane Willis has been a teacher of EFL in Ghana, Cyprus and Iran. She recently completed an M.A. in Applied Linguistics. Much of her work has been in teacher training but during 1981 she was a member of Aston University's Video Research Group investigating the applications of video to ELT. The two articles in this book are a result of the work of the research team.